W9-AZL-833

MRS MCSWEENEY
70 SHADYSIDE AVE
PORT WASHINGTO NY 11050

DISCARD

Mikhail Gorbachev

A Leader for Soviet Change

by Walter Oleksy

CHILDRENS PRESS®
CHICAGO

PICTURE ACKNOWLEDGMENTS

AP/Wide World Photos—Frontispiece, pages 28, 60 (bottom), 84, 85, 87
(top right), 88 (top right and bottom), 134
Sovfoto—8, 89 90
Reuters/Bettmann Newsphotos—40
Tass from Sovfoto—60 (top), 86, 87 (top left and bottom)
Eastfoto—88 (top left)
Cover illustration by Len W. Meents

LIBRARY OF CONGRESS
Library of Congress Cataloging-in-Publication Data

Olesky, Walter G., 1930-
  Mikhail Gorbachev (a leader for Soviet change) /
by Walter Olesky.
     p. cm.
  Includes index.
  Summary: Describes the life and rise to power of the
Soviet leader who has brought about the present openness
of the Soviet Union to the West.
  ISBN 0-516-03265-8
  1. Gorbachev, Mikhail Sergeevich, 1931-   —Juvenile
literature. 2. Heads of state—Soviet Union—Biography—
Juvenile literature. 3. Soviet Union—Politics and
government—1982-   —Juvenile literature.
[1. Gorbachev, Mikhail Sergeevich, 1931-   . 2. Heads of
state.] I. Title.
DK290.3.G67054   1989
947.085′4′0924—dc19
  [B]   88-36960
                                                           CIP
                                                            AC

Copyright © 1989 by Childrens Press®, Inc.
All rights reserved. Published simultaneously in Canada.
Printed in the United States of America.

  2 3 4 5 6 7 8 9 10 R 98 97 96 95 94 93 92 91 90 89

ACKNOWLEDGMENTS

The editors would like to acknowledge use of excerpted material from the following works:

From FROM RUSSIA TO USSR: A NARRATIVE AND DOCUMENTARY HISTORY by Janet G. Vaillant and John Richards II. Copyright © 1985 by Longman Inc. Reprinted by permission.

Let History Judge by Roy Medvedev. Copyright © by Roy Medvedev. Used by permission of Dr. Zhores A. Medvedev and David Jorasky.

The Associated Press, July 18, 1988; April 17, 1987.

Reprinted by permission of the H.W. Wilson Company from *Current Biography Yearbook 1985.* Copyright 1985, 1986 by the H.W. Wilson Company. All rights reserved.

Copyright 1986, 1987 by Newsweek, Inc. All Rights Reserved. Reprinted by permission.

From *A Time for Peace* by Mikhail S. Gorbachev. Copyright © 1985 by Mikhail Gorbachev. Published by arrangement with Richardson & Steirman.

From *The Coming Century of Peace* by Mikhail S. Gorbachev. Copyright © 1986 by Mikhail Gorbachev. Published by arrangement with Richardson & Steirman.

U.S. News & World Report, May 26, 1986; April 20, 1987; May 20, 1987; June 15, 1987.

The Christian Science Monitor, May 14, 1987; February 20, 1987; March 10, 1987; January 15, 1987; July 18, 1986.

Reprinted with permission of United Press International, Copyright 1986

© Copyrighted, Chicago Tribune Company, all rights reserved, used with permission.

Reuters, December 24, 1987. Reprinted by permission.

Table of Contents

Chapter 1

A NEW LEADER FOR THE SOVIET UNION

In the United States, when a president dies in office or a new president is elected by the people, an orderly and peaceful transition of power takes place.

In the largest country on earth, the Union of Soviet Socialist Republics, the highest-ranking leader is not a president but the general secretary of the Communist party that governs and runs the country.

In the Soviet Union, a change of general secretary has often resulted in a long power struggle. Many leaders of the Communist party would fight among themselves politically for the highest position.

So when General Secretary Konstantin Chernenko died on March 11, 1985, it was a great surprise that a successor was named so swiftly.

That man, Mikhail S. Gorbachev, a stocky, balding, friendly-faced son of peasants, came to power with a minimum of political opposition or criticism.

What made the choice of Gorbachev so interesting to the West was that it appeared to signal a major change in Soviet political thinking. The previous general secretaries all had been men who had come to power under the old guard of

Soviet politicians. They had followed in the hard-line footsteps of Joseph Stalin, one of the most powerful and feared leaders of the Soviet Union. Under Stalin, life was hard for most Soviet citizens, and millions who complained during his regime were put in prison or killed.

While also a strong leader, Gorbachev appeared to be a more moderate man, not a stern, frowning, angry leader. He was associated with a transfer of power from the old generation of Soviet leaders to a younger, better educated, more liberal, and open-minded type of leader.

Many Western observers saw Gorbachev's rise to power as a welcome breath of fresh air in what had become a rather static, predictable attitude by the Soviet leaders.

Mikhail Gorbachev seemed to be a man who would be a more enlightened, reasonable Soviet leader. The West might hope to deal with him on more rational terms. He might not automatically be against every idea, just because it came from the West.

Whether the West could deal with General Secretary Gorbachev was a matter that only time would tell. But early signs were that he was making an effort to be reasonable on major world issues, such as nuclear arms control. He also spent much of his first years in power trying to bring positive change to his country. He appeared to be more open and willing to discuss issues, such as human rights, with the West.

When Gorbachev took control, the country needed to become more economically sound. Many also felt it should be more politically and socially free. Shortages existed in everything from food to clothing and housing. Morale among Soviets had been low for years, because each general secretary had promised a higher standard of living, if the people would just work harder and do without a little longer—but trust their leaders. Years of hard work and trust and doing without did not bring the changes the Soviet people had been promised in the past.

Gorbachev introduced social, political, and economic reforms in his first years in power—without being too liberal. If he tried to bring too much change about too fast, he might lose the support he needed from other leaders in the Communist party and he might be removed from office. In the Soviet Union, there is always political jockeying for power.

Besides internal reforms, Gorbachev also had to work toward similar reforms in the Soviet "satellite" countries such as Poland, Yugoslavia, Czechoslovakia, and Hungary. And he had to deal with the West on arms control, nuclear power, war tensions in the Middle East and Central and South America, human rights, and other issues.

It is reported that most people in the Soviet Union spend about one-third of their life standing in line with a "maybe bag," waiting to buy something. They don't care what is for sale. They either need it or will buy it so they can trade it for something they do need or want.

The Soviet people also have been standing in line for years for some things even more important to them than new shoes, TV sets, or refrigerators. They have been longing for social, political, and religious freedoms. They do not enjoy many of the freedoms that people of many other countries take for granted, such as the freedom of speech or freedom to travel.

Mikhail Gorbachev was the first Soviet leader to offer the people some hope for real change. He told the people that change for the better was not only possible, but essential for the country to become more healthy and prosperous.

Shortly after becoming general secretary, Gorbachev began talking of the need for his country to develop "new thinking" in both domestic matters and international relations. The winds of change were soon in the air. Gorbachev began using a Russian word, *glasnost*, which means "openness." He said glasnost would help bring about the necessary changes.

An openness was needed to throw open the windows that had been closed in the Soviet Union and let in the fresh air of criticism, honesty, and fairness. Citizens could speak out without fearing they would be sent to prison or shot.

The Soviet leader also began to call for *perestroika*, which means not only reform but "restructuring." Gorbachev told his country's government leaders and the people that in order to bring about necessary change and improvements in all areas of domestic life, reforms would have to be made in everything from agriculture to industry, from education to housing. The nation's entire political and societal system would have to be restructured to make everything work better.

This new general secretary was taking a big job upon himself. But he appeared to be a man of great courage, with new ideas and determination to bring positive change to his people and his country.

Chapter 2

A BOY OF THE RUSSIAN REVOLUTION

Only fourteen years after the Russian Revolution, Mikhail Sergeyevich Gorbachev was born on March 2, 1931. His birthplace was the village of Privolnoye in Stavropol territory. It is a vast, rich agricultural region in southern Russia, just north of the Caucasus Mountains.

Mikhail's father was a peasant. Mikhail might have grown up to be like his father and grandfather, poor men who worked the land and did the czar's bidding. If they refused to do anything their imperial masters wished, or even criticized their wishes or orders, they likely would have been thrown into prison, sent to a labor camp in Siberia, or killed.

But the revolution brought hope to the Gorbachev family and millions of others. As a citizen of the new Union of Soviet Socialist Republics, young Mikhail would have to work just as hard, perhaps even harder, than under the czar. But at least he would be part of a country with a new beginning, with a sense of hope for new freedom and prosperity.

The Soviet Union was born out of a revolution led by the Bolsheviks, a Communist group. Vladimir Ilyich Lenin and other political activists, fed up with the imperial rule of Czar Nicholas II, seized power.

Reasons for the revolution were many and went back centuries. The land earlier had been called Russia, after the "Rus" Vikings from the Baltic lands whose leader Rurik founded the city of Novgorod in A.D. 862. Later, in 1200, the Mongol warlord Genghis Khan and his armies ruled the land.

In 1547 Ivan the Terrible, the czar of Russia, began the pattern of life for the people that continued until the 1917 revolution. The Russians lived in terror and poverty for almost four hundred years.

In 1613, the first czar from the royal family of Romanov came to power. The Romanovs ruled—with little or no concern for the plight of the people—until the revolution.

During those hard years, the czars and their political and economic friends lived in luxury at the expense of the people. The vast majority of Russians were poor farmers who lived in terrible poverty and had no political rights. Most of them could neither read nor write and were kept ignorant on purpose, so they could be easily controlled by their leaders.

Mikhail Gorbachev was born into a different world than his father or grandfather had known. It was not an easy life, but at least the Romanovs were out of power and there was a new and different leadership. It had been a people's uprising and after the revolution, the people could expect a change for the better. It was impossible to think that things could be any worse. The country was still poor, and everyone would have to work hard to improve their lot. But at least now there was hope for a better future.

The Gorbachevs and most other families in the Stavropol region were better off than most others in the country. They did not live in poverty or suffer the hardships of many others. Serfdom, which had been abolished in 1861, had not reached as far as Stavropol. It was a form of slavery in which peasants worked on the land of royal landowners for little or no pay. They seldom had enough to eat and lived in housing little better than the barns for the horses or cows. In Stavropol, peasants were fortunate enough to live as free farmers and there was enough land and food for everyone.

Life, however, was not all that safe or easy for the Gorbachevs from the time of the revolution until Mikhail's birth and even afterward.

The region was the scene of fierce fighting for three years after the revolution. It was a time of civil war when the Bolsheviks ("Red" Russians) fought the Cossacks ("White" Russians) in a power struggle for control of the country. The Bolsheviks won in 1920, but it did not bring an end to misfortune.

The next year, a terrible drought caused crops to fail and the region suffered from famine. More than five million people died from starvation or disease from 1921 to 1922.

Mikhail's village was close to the area hit hardest by the

famine and sickness. His parents saw thousands of people from the stricken area pass through Privolnoye on their way farther north to more fertile regions.

Now began hard times for the people of Stavropol. From 1922 until Mikhail was born almost ten years later, the Soviet Union's leader was Joseph Stalin. He was the first Communist dictator and brought about a reign of terror and misfortune that the people had never known before, even under the czars.

Stalin's New Economic Policy for the country was to encourage increased farming and make the Soviet Union a more industrialized nation. Peasants everywhere hailed his farm policy and it was not long before farmers were producing abundantly. The North Caucasus again became a major food producing region for the whole country and led in grain production.

Then, dissatisfied with farming methods that were still for the most part centuries old and inefficient, Stalin tried something new. It was to have far-reaching and terrible effects on the people and the country. He began a system of collective farming and placed more emphasis on industrialization. Conditions became even harder than war had been.

"The Soviet Union must march forward so that the world proletariat can look to it as the true fatherland of the working class," Stalin said in 1931. "We are fifty or one hundred years behind the advanced countries. We must make good this distance in ten years. Either we do it, or we shall be crushed."[1]

Wealthier farmers began resisting the policy and Stalin began a campaign to have them eliminated as a social class. Their farms were taken from them and those who resisted collective farming were sent to forced labor camps in Siberia or were executed. Between three and five million people died because of the collective farming campaign or from the famine that resulted from it.

A major effect of collective farming was to "dehumanize" the people. They had been regarded as no better than animals under the czars. Now the Soviets in power considered them to be just as expendable. They were to be used as needed or to be put away or killed.

But Stalin's plan called for fewer farmers to work more efficient large farms using modern farming machinery the new factories would produce. The surplus of farmers would work in the factories to increase the industrial output of the new country. In theory it might have worked. In practice, it didn't.

During this reign of terror Mikhail Gorbachev was born. His father, Sergei Andreevich Gorbachev, was a machine operator in a local tractor station. Later he became a minor official in the district's Communist party. He died in 1976. Little is known of Mikhail's mother, Maria Panteleyvna, who was seventy-six years old in 1988 and living in Privolnoye.

The name of the village means "free" and "spacious," because it lies in the sparsely populated farming country close to the arid steppe, and because most of the farmers there were free men and not serfs.

Mikhail's birthplace is part of the vast North Caucasian territory between the Azov, Black, and Caspian seas. The village dates from the late eighteenth century when the southern plains of Russia were colonized by peasants. Earlier, in the sixteenth and seventeenth centuries, peasant-soldiers called cossacks had settled in the area.

Not much is known of Mikhail's boyhood or youth, except that he grew up as a typical country boy of his times. He was born during the first year of the first Five-Year Plan of Joseph Stalin. Stalin was certain that the Soviet Union's future lay in developing its industry like the nations of the Western world. Cities and factory workers were important to him.

But Mikhail Gorbachev was born into a part of the new Soviet Union that was farm country, not a city with industry. It is significant today because Gorbachev, who loves his rural birthplace, apparently has not lost his close ties to the people, to farming, and to the rural life of his parents and grandparents. A love of the land runs deep in a Soviet citizen's heart. The land is still like a mother and the country is still called "Mother Russia."

Something else that runs deep in the Soviet nature is an

historic distrust of foreigners. The country had been over-run by many foreign invaders over the centuries, from the Mongols to the French under Napoleon and the Germans under Hitler during World War II.

It is no wonder the Soviets distrust foreigners. So for centuries, the people preferred to be blissfully isolated from the rest of the world. To a large extent, this mistrust of foreigners and preferred isolation has kept the nation from growing sufficiently to become a part of the rest of the world.

The Soviet Union in which Mikhail Gorbachev was born in 1931 was almost like a different planet from what lay beyond its borders. It would be years before Mikhail would know that another world existed.

Chapter 3

A YOUTH OF THE NEW SOVIET UNION

The inevitable came to the village of Privolnoye in the spring when Mikhail Gorbachev was born. A *kolkholz*, a collective farm, was established in the area. Mikhail's grandfather spoke in favor of the new collective farm and soon became its chairman. His parents joined the collective and worked to produce more grain for the hungry nation.

Stalin's first Five-Year Plan was called a success when the industrial output of 1931 was 21 percent greater than that of the previous year. Most of the gain was in heavy industry and machine tools.

But the same success could not be said of the collective farms. Production lagged, workers rebelled as best they could in what were called "grain strikes," and a nationwide food shortage persisted.

A new pattern had begun. Forced labor in collectives and farmers forced to work in factories resulted in a growing lack of incentive among workers in both occupations. This problem exists even today in the Soviet Union, as people are forced to work in jobs other than ones they would choose for themselves if they could.

Despite all the five-year production plans that followed,

prosperity never came. Shortages of food and clothing—even basics such as toilet paper—persist. Most products manufactured in Soviet factories, such as shoes, television sets, or automobiles are poorly made. They tend to wear out or break down too fast.

Even in the 1980s, morale among workers continues to be low, mainly because the system does not work. Stalin and his successors were never able to make things better.

Stalin was especially disturbed about the low grain production in the Stavropol region. In October 1932, he sent a special team there to investigate the problem. The commission was given great powers and placed the area under a state of emergency.

While Mikhail was too young to suffer directly during this time of trouble, his family and others suffered. Most families lost relatives or friends who were sent to labor camps or executed. Their crime, whether actual or not, was that they were "malicious saboteurs," or shirkers, who did not want to work on the collective farms.

The winters of 1932-33 and 1933-34, when Mikhail was two and three years old, were ones of hardship and famine for the people of the Stavropol area, just as it was for most of the southern part of the country. Those who suffered most were the children. In some nearby villages, all the children between the ages of one and two died of hunger or sickness. Mikhail Gorbachev was one of the lucky ones. He survived.

A Soviet writer, A.B. Kosterin, who visited the North Caucasus in 1933 and 1934, wrote this about what he saw: "I had the occasion to go through dozens of villages in Stavropol . . . [I saw] Houses with boarded-up windows, empty barnyards, abandoned equipment in fields. And terrifying mortality, especially among children . . .

"On the deserted road to Stavropol I met a peasant with a knapsack. We stopped, greeted each other, had a smoke. I asked him, 'Where are you tramping, comrade?'

"'To prison.'

"Astonishment kept me from saying or asking anything. I only looked my amazement at the old man. . . . He smoked calmly and quite unexcitedly told me his story. He was a middle peasant who had been sentenced to ten years. . . . for refusing to join a collective farm and for speaking against the plenipotentiary [official] in the village meeting. The village policeman lacked the time or the inclination to escort him to Stavropol, so he was going alone."[1]

It is likely that Mikhail Gorbachev heard similar stories as he was growing up. The hardships of his peasant relatives and friends had a lasting effect on him. It is a major reason why as general secretary he had not lost touch with his home region and the farming people there. He appeared to have a genuine feeling of compassion for all the people.

When Mikhail was five years old, Stalin made some changes that later were called the "Stalin Constitution" of

1936. In an administrative rearrangement of the Soviet Union, the North Caucasus political structure was divided into several regional bodies. Part of the reorganization resulted in the arrest and execution of many local officials who were accused of not performing as was expected.

Stavropol was something of an ethnic melting pot when Mikhail was growing up. A large area of about thirty-one thousand square miles, it was mostly farming country. Most of the people living in the region were Russian, but there also were some Muslims in the mountain regions. So Mikhail grew up seeing some foreigners and talking to them, starting to understand their differences and similarities.

Mikhail was eight years old when a rising political leader named Mikhail Suslov was appointed first secretary of Stavropol's *kraikom*, its political governing body. Also of peasant origin, Suslov had been a member of the Communist party since 1921. Later he worked for the Party in Moscow.

Suslov had a reputation for carrying out the Party's often ruthless orders, including the arrest of everyone in some political agencies. Years later, Suslov was to play an important role in helping Mikhail Gorbachev up the ladder of political success. Suslov helped him become secretary of the Central Committee of the Soviet Party.

Like most Soviet children between the ages of eight and twelve, most of Mikhail's boyhood centered around school.

Starting in the late 1920s, children went to primary schools. Most villages had such a school.

Larger villages, such as Privolnoye, also had "pre-secondary" schools for those aged twelve to fifteen, which Mikhail would later attend. After graduation from pre-secondary school, most children of peasants were expected to begin working on a collective farm at the age of sixteen, unless they were lucky enough to continue their education at a secondary school.

Mikhail was ten years old, attending primary school, when the German army invaded the Soviet Union, in June of 1941. Mikhail's father and all other men in the village in their twenties or thirties were taken into the Soviet army.

In August, with the advance of the German "blitzkrieg," a fierce offensive, Nazi troops entered Stavropol, about two hundred miles from Privolnoye. But though the German occupation lasted five months, Soviet resistance kept the Nazis from advancing farther into the North Caucasus.

Mikhail waited anxiously, but his home village never became a battle zone. The Nazis bypassed Privolnoye, instead destroying towns and villages situated along railways or more strategic roads.

Mikhail wanted to study, to learn more about everything. But he had to drop out of pre-secondary school for a year in 1942, when he was eleven, to help with the war effort in the area. In the fall of 1943, he resumed his studies.

Years later, Mikhail's mother said the war years were hard on the family, with Mikhail's father away fighting the Nazis.

"In 1944, Misha [his mother's pet name for Mikhail] was in fifth grade. He couldn't go to school [for three months] because he didn't have shoes."

When she wrote his father about this, he told her to "sell whatever you can, but buy shoes for Misha. He must study."

Maria Gorbachev said she "went to the market and sold whatever I could, and with the money I earned, I bought a pair of combat boots . . . and I took him to school."

The headmaster didn't think Mikhail could catch up after falling behind three months. But young Misha promised, "I'll make it up,"[2] and he earned his diploma with honors.

Mikhail's father returned home after having been wounded in Czechoslovakia and getting treatment in a Polish hospital. Sergei recovered and worked in the fields where Mikhail helped by operating a combine.

By the time the war ended in 1945, more than eighteen million Russians had been killed.

From 1945 Mikhail worked summers as a temporary employee of the local machine-tractor station. He became an assistant combine harvest operator. His work at the tractor station took the place of working for a kolkholz. But it was just as hard work as farming and he often put in twelve-hour workdays.

When he turned eighteen in 1949, Mikhail began a two-stage process toward becoming a member of the Communist party. He became a candidate member for one year. It was a probationary period that allowed him to attend Party meetings and expected him to obey Party laws. It did not give him voting privileges.

Hard work paid off for Mikhail and others in Privolnoye. The harvest of 1949 exceeded its quota. Many local officials and workers were given awards. Mikhail was awarded the Order of the Red Banner of Labor from the Presidium of the Supreme Soviet. It was quite an honor for a teenage peasant.

After his probationary year, for all practical purposes, Mikhail was a member of the Communist party by 1950. However, he did not become a full member until 1952.

His schooling delayed a year by his war work, Mikhail graduated from secondary school in June 1950. At graduation, he was awarded a silver medal for excellence. He also was given another honor, the opportunity of entering an institution of higher education. Not many boys his age were given this chance. But the honor had its risks. If he failed his entrance exams, he would have to go into the army.

Mikhail went for it. He had gotten the government award for his factory work, the graduation award, and had become a candidate member of the Communist party. These successes gave him the courage to apply to the most prestigious institution in the Soviet Union—Moscow State University.

Mikhail Gorbachev, almost twenty years old, wears the Red Banner of Labor medal he earned for driving a harvest combine.

Chapter 4

THE RISE OF A YOUNG SOVIET

Mikhail could hardly believe his good fortune as he rode in a train to his nation's capital, Moscow. The farmlands of his youth passed by his window, but his thoughts were not on them. They were of the future and of the great city where the train was headed and his life in the university.

His excitement can be understood. He was only nineteen, the son of peasants from a remote part of the country. No one in his family had ever gone to a university.

He knew why he was going. He had worked hard in school, for the war effort, and then in the farm factory. And though he was new in the Communist party, he felt that his loyalty and willingness to work for it were already being recognized and rewarded.

At first he thought he would study physics. Then he changed his mind and decided to study law. But he apparently did not intend to practice law. It was not a prestigious field of study at that time in the Soviet Union. When he decided to study law, it was mainly in order to prepare for higher work in the Communist party.

As a student in the law school at Moscow State University, Mikhail began to put more of his energy into politics than his studies. His country's future lay with the success of the Party, he believed, and so too did his future.

The government gave university students a small amount of money to live on, but it was barely enough to provide their meals. Mikhail's parents could not give him much, but the Party helped him. Unlike many others who lived in crowded dormitories at the university, Mikhail shared a double room. His roommate was Zdenek Mlynar, a young man from Czechoslovakia.

Mlynar, who became active in his own country's Communist party, wrote later about the five years he and Gorbachev were roommates. They were in the same study group, took the same examinations, and were awarded the same degrees.

According to Mlynar, Gorbachev was a loyal and honest young man. He was intelligent without being arrogant, and carried himself with a natural air of authority. He said Gorbachev did not have a lot of original ideas, but made an effort to be everybody's friend.

Mlynar noticed one important thing in young Mikhail. Even in 1952 when they were studying together, twenty-one-year-old Gorbachev at times questioned the decisions of Joseph Stalin. He took opposing views on some issues and especially disagreed that anyone who criticized Stalin or his orders was a traitor to the Party and should be sent to a labor camp or executed.

It was brave but dangerous to hold such views or talk

about them then. But Gorbachev thought that the people should be allowed to voice their opinions about anything without being afraid.

While Mlynar saw Gorbachev as a popular student, others saw him differently. One said Gorbachev at times spoke out angrily about classmates who told disloyal stories or shirked being sent to a collective farm.

Gorbachev returned each summer to Privolnoye to work as a combine operator. He earned extra money for the next school year. He also reinforced his dedication to Stalin and the Party's collective farm system.

Besides attending lectures, reading, and taking exams, law students were required to take some practical training as law clerks, court clerks, or work in the militia or criminal investigation departments. Gorbachev chose to take his practical apprenticeship in the office of one of the country's best defense lawyers.

It was a rather controversial decision. Graduating law students who had trained in defense lawyers' offices usually were considered to be critical of the Communist party and therefore not trustworthy. Perhaps Gorbachev chose to study with a top defense attorney so he could learn the other side of the law as it existed under Stalin.

After joining the Communist party, Gorbachev became active in the Young Communist League, or *Komsomol*. It is the traditional training ground for Soviet party officials.

Five years passed and graduation day came. Gorbachev was not offered an opportunity to go on to graduate school, so he had to go through the process of finding a job. But he could not take just any job he wanted. He had to apply for one through the system of jobs appointed by the state.

Most graduates returned to their native cities or villages and started work there with the local Communist party. Gorbachev decided not to look for work as a defense lawyer. Instead he chose to work in the Komsomol and the Communist party.

He was especially qualified to work for the Young Communists because at law school he had proven himself to be an excellent speaker and related well to young people.

But though Gorbachev learned a great deal in law school and began a promising future in the Communist party, something else of significance came out of his university years and his friendship with his Czech roommate. Mlynar knew more about the rest of the world than most of the instructors at the university. Gorbachev learned from him about the West and it was at a time, in the early 1950s, when Joseph Stalin had kept the Soviet people virtually shut off from the Western world.

Some slightly older Party leaders who also made a point of knowing more about the West saw promise in young Gorbachev. New Party officials such as Suslov and Yuri Andropov, who later became general secretary of the Communist party from 1982 to 1984, began to notice him. They counted him among the select group of young Soviets who, like themselves, might breathe some new life into the Party. Perhaps they could lead it away from Stalin's rigid ways and turn it toward a more just and moderate system.

After graduating in June 1955, Gorbachev returned to Stavropol. He expected to be assigned to a local procuracy, the largest section of the legal system in the Soviet Union. The procuracy sees that the laws of the country are strictly observed by both citizens and organizations.

But most procurators' jobs were already overstaffed. The courts were crowded with cases against victims of Stalin's reign of terror. About ten million people had been convicted of crimes against the state and were in prison, though most of them might only have been overheard criticizing the government.

The best way Gorbachev could avoid going into this type of court work was to work instead for the Komsomol or the Party.

Gorbachev's first job with the Party was not an important one, especially for a new graduate of Moscow State University. He was assigned to be head of a department of the Stavropol City Komsomol Committee. Only a year later, he was made the first secretary of the committee.

Shortly before this promotion, Gorbachev got married. He had met Raisa Titorenko, an attractive young woman, when she also was studying at the university. She lived in the same student housing hostel where Gorbachev shared a room with Mlynar.

The young couple had several things in common. Raisa also came from Stavropol and had graduated from secondary school a year after Gorbachev. She later was graduated from Moscow State University's Department of Science with a degree in philosophy. First she worked as a teacher, then as a sociologist at the local teacher training institute. Today she is a senior lecturer in the university's philosophy department.

Some of Gorbachev's success in Stavropol had been credited to Raisa's influence and advice. In 1956, their only daughter, Irina, was born. Today Irina is a physician. Her husband, Anatoli, is a surgeon. They have a daughter, Ksenia, born in 1976.

Work with the Komsomol did not pay much and the young couple lived modestly. But Gorbachev liked his work with young people who were eager to join the Party. As a youth organization for those aged fourteen to twenty-seven, there were clubs and sports events and summer camps as well as lectures and meetings.

For the next four years, Gorbachev worked as first deputy chief of propaganda. Later he became Party organizer for the territorial production board of collective and state farms.

In 1963, Gorbachev became chief of the agricultural

department for the entire Stavropol region. It was an important post for a young man then only thirty-two years old. At the same time, he took courses in farm economics at the Stavropol Agricultural Institute and obtained a diploma in agronomy in 1967.

Gorbachev continued to rise in the Party. In 1970 he was named deputy to the Soviet of the Union within the Supreme Soviet, the formal legislative body of the Soviet Union. He was named to its conservation and youth affairs commissions, and became chairman of the youth commission in 1974.

In 1971 he had become a member of the powerful Central Committee. He served as a delegate to several Party congresses in the Soviet Union and was sent on trips abroad, heading Party delegations to Belgium, West Germany, and France.

But no matter how hard or steadfast Gorbachev, or any other young man in the Soviet Union worked for the Communist party, he did not get ahead without the help of mentors. Gorbachev was especially successful at attracting the favor of powerful men. His first mentor had been Mikhail Suslov, a former Stavropol Communist party chief who served later as ideology minister to General Secretary Leonid I. Brezhnev. But Gorbachev also gained the backing of the Suslov faction in the Kremlin, including Yuri Andropov, then chairman of the KGB, the Soviet secret police, and the agricultural minister, Fyodor Kulakov.

In 1978, Kulakov died of a heart attack. After the death of Kulakov, Gorbachev was named to replace him as secretary of agriculture. But the new position was as dangerous as it was enticing, because for a long time Soviet agriculture had been underproductive. The Five-Year Plans of other agricultural secretaries and general secretaries had failed. The causes for failure included limited amount of available arable land, uncertain climate, and problems of collective management of farms.

But unexpectedly, Gorbachev's farming background did not serve him well. He came up with an idea for a "brigade" system under which groups of workers were assigned to farm their individual plots.

The brigade plan was not, however, a success. During Gorbachev's tenure in agriculture, harvests were so poor the government stopped publishing crop statistics. It had to spend billions of dollars to buy grain from the United States and other countries.

Despite his lack of success in agriculture, Gorbachev continued to rise in the Communist party, with the influence of his political patrons and because he was considered a young man of promise and loyalty. In 1979 he became a nonvoting member of the Politburo or "political bureau," a small group of leading Communist party members who control the government. The next year, he became the youngest member of the Central Committee's policy-making body.

This period was difficult for the Soviet leadership. General Secretary Leonid Brezhnev, already elderly, grew ill and was unable to rule effectively. Corruption in the government became widespread.

When Brezhnev died in 1982, the reform element in the Kremlin elected Yuri Andropov as general secretary. He immediately started a wide-ranging program of reform.

As Andropov's right-hand man, Gorbachev was Andropov's assistant and helped to carry out his mentor's reform initiatives. They included exposing corrupt and incompetent Party officials. This purge resulted in the removal of one-fifth of the regional Party secretaries, one-third of their staffs, and thousands of local managers and Party workers.

Gorbachev also was put in charge of supervising Andropov's programs, begun in January 1984, to start decentralization and technological change in a small number of industries.

As Andropov's health grew worse, Gorbachev became more visible in the government and the country, acting as his representative with other Party leaders. He made many speeches in Andropov's place and attended many important diplomatic meetings and functions.

In 1983, Gorbachev led a Soviet delegation to Canada. At this time, many observers began to believe Andropov was grooming Gorbachev as his successor. But when Andropov died, the older and more conservative Party members passed up young Gorbachev and elected another elderly Party leader, Konstantin Chernenko, as general secretary in February 1984. Chernenko was a Brezhnev loyalist and they apparently suspected Gorbachev was too young and inexperienced or might even be too liberal.

Gorbachev soon began to play important roles in Chernenko's administration. Early in 1984 he became chairman of the important areas of ideology, economics, and Party organization. In April he became chairman of the foreign affairs committee of the Supreme Soviet. While loyally supporting Chernenko, Gorbachev gradually took over more and more of the ailing chairman's functions.

One observer said Gorbachev was smart enough not to push Chernenko out. He just waited for the old man to drop.

In December of 1984, Gorbachev scored his first major victory outside the Soviet Union. He led a Soviet delegation on an exchange visit to the British Houses of Parliament, accompanied by his equally or perhaps even more charming wife. Her fashion and wit captivated many people and Gorbachev himself demonstrated a sense of humor. He also was found to be intelligent, quick to speak out on controversial issues, and to have a sophisticated style that appealed to a wide audience. On this trip Prime Minister Margaret Thatcher, a staunch anti-Communist, was so impressed with him, she remarked, "I like Mr. Gorbachev. We can do business together."[1]

Only a few hours after the death of Chernenko on March 11, 1985, the veteran foreign minister, Andrei Gromyko, nominated Gorbachev and he was elected general secretary in an emergency meeting. His election happened so fast, it convinced Soviet observers that it had been arranged long in advance.

While on a visit to Romania in 1987, Gorbachev joins in a Romanian folk dance.

Chapter 5

OPENNESS AND CHANGE

On March 12, 1985, Mikhail Gorbachev became the political leader of nearly 277 million people of more than 100 nationalities in the largest country in the world.

In his acceptance speech, Gorbachev emphasized the need for rapid economic development. He said it would be the most important goal of his administration. He also called for further perfection and development of democratic and socialist self-government.

Gorbachev also pledged to maintain the defense capacity of the motherland. As the same time, he urged that nuclear arms control talks resume with the United States.

He said his nation was not striving to acquire unilateral advantages over the United States and NATO (the North Atlantic Treaty Organization) powers. He promised to follow the Leninist course of peaceful coexistence with the United States and other Western nations.

At age fifty-four, Gorbachev became the youngest Soviet leader since Stalin succeeded Lenin in 1924. He was not only much younger than any of his predecessors, he looked a lot more friendly. He did something few Soviet leaders before him had ever done—he smiled.

Basically, Mikhail Gorbachev's personality and style of leadership charmed the people. The Soviets were not accustomed to this. From the start of his administration, he became a more public figure than his predecessors had been. He was seen often on television talking among the people, the workers. He asked what they wanted for their future. He encouraged them to complain and promised they would not be punished if they criticized him, the government, or their bosses.

A breath of fresh air had begun blowing across the country. There was a lot of hard work ahead, if Gorbachev were to bring about positive change.

Glasnost soon became the main focus of most of Gorbachev's speeches and policies. He also wanted to encourage more private enterprise in which people could own their own businesses and enjoy a profit, like Westerners. There was little of this in the Soviet Union. The government owned all the businesses and stores and the people worked for them.

In Gorbachev's first speeches as general secretary, he promised the people a wide range of changes that would make life better for them. He pledged economic and social changes that would allow them greater freedoms than they had ever lived under in the past.

Shortly after taking office, Gorbachev invited twenty-five Soviet writers to a private meeting in the Kremlin. He asked them to join him in fighting a common enemy: the middle-level bureaucrats who resisted his efforts to bring about economic, social, and political change. He told the writers that his plan to counter these bureaucrats and their objections was to begin a policy of openness.

"We don't have an opposition," Gorbachev told the writers, meaning that the government runs the country without anyone objecting to its policies and laws. "How then can we monitor ourselves? Only through criticism and self-criticism. And most of all through glasnost."[1]

Glasnost soon became almost a battle cry across the Soviet Union. The people were not used to being promised openness. They were not used to being encouraged to speak out against existing laws, policies, and government officials—or bosses who treated them unfairly.

Now Gorbachev was telling the people they no longer had to keep their grievances to themselves or to whisper them. They did not have to fear they would be punished if they spoke out about anything. Glasnost was Gorbachev's intended means to open a society that had been closed for decades. It would force bureaucrats and industrial leaders to be held accountable for their failures or any illegal practices. It would encourage hope in young people who had grown to expect their superiors to be corrupt and unfair.

"Our enemy [the United States] has figured us out," Gorbachev told Communist party leaders. "They are not frightened of our nuclear might. They are not going to start a war. They are worried about one thing: if democracy develops under us—if that happens, then we will win."[2]

Gorbachev's meaning of democracy might mean sweeping political and social changes for the average Soviet citizen. It does not mean democracy as we know it in the United States. It might be a giant step away from the corrupt and inefficient old system of Soviet government. But it would not be democracy with the freedoms Americans and other democratic nations enjoy.

Instead of complete political freedom, which Gorbachev may not have wanted and knew his critics would oppose, he intended encouraging individual creativity and initiative. It would give the people some hope for a better future, and they might work harder and better. Only through such effort would the Soviet Union solve its economic problems and become a stronger, healthier nation.

The health of the people was important to Gorbachev, not only politically and socially, but physically. Food production continued to be below that which was necessary to feed the millions of citizens. Basic consumer goods that would allow the people to live adequately were in short supply. A sense of desperation had driven many people to alcoholism, drug abuse, and prostitution. Absenteeism from jobs caused serious economic problems.

Another word the people began hearing from Gorbachev

was "change." He said he wanted to bring about many changes to make life better for the people. Changes were needed in the economic, social, and political system. Gorbachev urged the other leaders and the people to support his program of changes.

The changes Gorbachev hoped to bring about would not come easily. First of all, he inherited many problems from his predecessors. The country was not working efficiently.

Secondly, Gorbachev did not have absolute power. He would be allowed only the power he could manage to get from the Politburo, the leaders of the Communist party. Many of these leaders worried about Gorbachev's speeches calling for openness and change. Their power might be jeopardized if the people were allowed to criticize them or bring them to account for their actions.

The third problem Gorbachev would have in bringing about openness and change was the people themselves. They had lived for years under a system in which one could be severely punished for speaking against anything or anyone. Many were fearful. They did not trust Gorbachev's promise not to be harmed if they spoke out. Many others were simply fearful of change. Bad as things had been and were, maybe it would be better to stay with old ways rather than risk change.

Change was unfamiliar. The Soviet people had been taught to follow their leaders, whether they liked it or not.

They had learned to become good followers. Changing and being allowed to play a role in their future was, to many people, frightening. They would rather follow than step out of ranks and join a parade that might single them out as complainers or troublemakers.

But Gorbachev decided for the good of his people to try to bring about social, political, and economic changes and openness.

Chapter 6

A CALL FOR REFORM

Most of the problems Gorbachev inherited were basic. The job of government, according to the Soviet constitution, is to see to it that the people work for the good of each other and the country. This is accomplished by shaping the thinking and attitude of each citizen, as well as their behavior.

"The goal of the Soviet government is . . . to create 'the new Soviet man [and woman],' a new type of person free from greed and selfishness, laziness, and dishonesty."[1] With such people, a truly Communist society can result.

While most Americans would rebel against such a government, many Soviets not only go along with such a system, but prefer it. Many older Soviets who have spent a lifetime being told what to do and what to think do not believe that they would be better off if they took a more active role in the governing of their lives. They prefer a leadership that will organize everyone in an orderly way to work for a common goal, a goal set by the Communist party. Since such free reign of government is welcomed, the government and Communist party reaches into many corners of Soviet life.

On March 11, 1985, the day before he was named general secretary, Gorbachev spoke at a special meeting of the Party's Central Committee.

Doubtless his words influenced his election: "In the foreign-policy sphere, our course is clear and consistent. It is the course of peace and progress," Gorbachev vowed.

In dealing with the United States and other capitalist states, Gorbachev pledged to "... firmly follow the Leninist course of peace and peaceful coexistence. The Soviet Union will always respond to goodwill with goodwill, to trust with trust. But everyone should know that we shall never relinquish the interests of our Motherland and those of our allies."

Then Gorbachev addressed the nuclear arms race issue: "Never before has so terrible a threat hung over mankind as now," he said. "The only reasonable way out of the existing situation is for the opposing forces to reach an agreement on the immediate termination of the arms race—the nuclear arms race on earth and the prevention of an arms race in space. . . . We need an agreement that would help everyone advance toward the cherished goal—the complete elimination and prohibition of nuclear weapons for all time—toward the complete removal of the threat of nuclear war. This is our firm conviction."[2]

On March 22, ten days after becoming general secretary, and on the eve of arms talks in Geneva, Switzerland, Gorbachev met in the Kremlin with members of the Advisory Council on Disarmament of the Socialist International. He proposed a freeze on both Soviet and United States nuclear arsenals and an end to the further deployment of missiles.

United States Congressman Thomas "Tip" O'Neill, then speaker of the House of Representatives, heading a delegation from the House, visited the Kremlin at the invitation of the Supreme Soviet. Gorbachev welcomed O'Neill and the opportunity for leaders of both countries to talk and do what they could to improve Soviet-American relations. Gorbachev emphasized that the Soviet leadership sincerely wished that Soviet-American relations would return to normalcy.

"We do not think that behind present tensions in these relations is some fatal clash of national interests," Gorbachev told O'Neill. "On the contrary, our peoples can gain much from the development of broad and fruitful cooperation, to say nothing of the fact that they are united by the dominating common interest of ensuring security and preserving the very life of our peoples. The difference in social systems, in the ideology of our countries is no cause for curtailing relations, much less for kindling hatred."

But Gorbachev challenged United States figures indicating the Soviets had more nuclear weapons than the United States and its allies. He insisted "that, in reality, there is parity, or a rough balance between the Soviet Union and the NATO countries in all of these weapons."

He went on to urge "an end to a further buildup of the nuclear arsenals on earth, halt preparations for the creation of weapons for deployment in outer space, and . . . under the conditions of mutual trust . . . immediately begin preparing agreements to reduce the accumulated weapons stocks." To accomplish this, Gorbachev declared that the Soviet Union was "unilaterally halting further deployment of its medium range missiles and suspending the implementation of other countermeasures in Europe until November of this year."[3]

Thus began a new series of proposals on arms reduction that continues to this day.

On the eve of the fortieth anniversary of the end of World War II, Gorbachev paid tribute to his countrymen who fought and died in that war. Then, on April 23, reporting to the Central Committee of the Communist Party, he turned to economic issues.

He accused the United States of manipulating interest rates, "plundering" activities of corporations with branches in many parts of the world, and political restrictions in trade. Also boycotts and sanctions that "are creating a climate of tension and mistrust in international economic relations . . ."[4] He said these policies were destabilizing the world economy and trade.

"We . . . advocate the development of normal, equal relations with capitalist countries," said Gorbachev. "All controversial issues and conflict situations should be resolved through political means—this is our firm conviction."[5]

But Gorbachev recognized that all his country's economic problems could not be blamed on the United States.

"... How and with what resources will the country be able to accelerate economic development?" Gorbachev asked the Party Central Committee. He said that he and members of the Politburo "... have unanimously arrived at the conclusion that real possibilities for this exist. The task of accelerating the rates of growth, and a substantial growth at that, is quite feasible if we place at the focus of all our work the intensification of the economy and acceleration of scientific and technological progress, if we carry out a reorganization of management, planning and the structural and investment policy, if we raise the efficiency of organization and strengthen discipline everywhere and if we basically improve the style of our work."[6]

This speech pointed to Gorbachev's overall plan to rework the Soviet economic system to make it function more efficiently. It would mean stepping on a lot of toes, but for the good of the country, broad economic changes were imperative.

"It is possible to obtain relatively quick results if we put organizational-economic, and social reserves to work and above all if we activate the human factor, i.e. make sure that every person works on his job conscientiously and to the best of his ability."[7]

His plan would call for not only factory workers but also farmers on the collective and state farms to work harder. It also would mean that supervisors would have to work harder and more efficiently and, though not directly stated, more honestly.

Gorbachev also pointed out the problems of waste and losses, accusing some executives in industry and government of being irresponsible. In factories, equipment sometimes stays idle or is not used to its fullest, he asserted.

Construction was taking too long, and the building of homes and factories was being delayed or jeopardized by inefficient building practices.

"It is necessary to make persons who are responsible for the proper storage and correct utilization of all material values more strictly answerable," Gorbachev said, "legally answerable for their work. Good order must be established at every enterprise and construction site, at every collective and state farm, at every organization. Without this there can be no talk about any kind of rational economic management or the growth of the economy's efficiency."[8]

This part of Gorbachev's speech pointed to a new policy in the Soviet Union, to hold executives accountable for their inefficient or illegal methods. Later this would be expanded to encourage citizens and workers to report grievances against their supervisors and any mismanagement or self gain of which they themselves might be guilty.

Gorbachev then called for replacement of much of his country's outdated and worn equipment in the factories and on the farms. He proposed new machines and equipment that could "ensure the introduction of progressive technology, raise productivity several times over, reduce the amount of material required per unit of output and increase the returns on assets."[9]

He also said, "It is time to start streamlining the organizational structures of management, to do away with unnecessary management bodies, to simplify the apparatus and raise its efficiency."[10] He also criticized the amount of government instructions and regulations that slow production.

Gorbachev went on to make suggestions to improve the quality of life for all Soviets. This could be accomplished through a renewed effort to increase food production, improve public health and education including school reform, improve communication with the people, and more freedom for the press, TV, and radio to organize and educate the masses and for shaping public opinion. He also hinted at allowing more creativity and freedom to writers of books, plays, and motion pictures. "There is no doubt that the new tasks which are being tackled today will find a befitting response in the creative endeavor which affirms the truth of socialist life. . . .

"The Party and the Soviet people expect from us comprehensive, well-thought-out and responsible decisions," Gorbachev said in closing his speech to the Central Committee. "And it can be said in all confidence that they will be supported by the Communists and by all the people. This support will find its expression in their social awareness, their activity and their work."[11]

On May 20, Gorbachev met with Malcolm Baldridge, then United States secretary of commerce, who had come to Moscow as head of a United States delegation to meet with the Soviet-American Commercial Commission.

Baldridge delivered to Gorbachev a letter from President Ronald Reagan expressing interest in expanding trade between the United States and the Soviet Union.

Gorbachev responded by saying that the unsatisfactory state of Soviet-American trade and economic ties were a result of the Reagan administration's policies. He accused the United States of discrimination against the Soviet Union, interfering in Soviet internal affairs, and using trade as a means of political pressure. He referred to a series of trade and cultural restrictions the United States had placed on the Soviet Union in the past few years. They were largely in opposition to the Soviet's foreign policy, including its aggression in Afghanistan and involvement in Central American countries, as well as human rights issues such as refusing to let Soviet Jews leave the country if they wished.

Gorbachev again recommended both nations freeze or curb the nuclear arms race and "the escalation of hostility." He said, "The main goal is to restore the climate of mutual trust in relations between our countries."[12]

Over the next months, Gorbachev continued his domestic programs for openness and change and spelled them out in more detail.

On July 27, he addressed young people who had gathered at the twelfth World Festival of Youth and Students, which was held in Moscow. He promised the young people from many countries that, "with all certainty . . . a world without wars and weapons, a world of good-neighborliness and cooperation in good faith, a world of friendship among nations are the ideals of socialism, the goals of our policy."[13]

Gorbachev again urged normal relations, mutual trust, and an end to the arms race when meeting with United States Senators Robert Byrd, Strom Thurmond, Sam Nunn, John Warner, and others who had come to the Kremlin that September 3. They had come at the invitation of the Parliamentary Group of the Soviet Union.

"The positions of our two countries on a number of issues do not coincide, which is predetermined by the major differences between our two systems," said Gorbachev. "But however deep these differences may be, they should not and cannot obstruct the main goal: our responsibility for averting the nuclear threat, for preserving peace."[14]

The senators said they welcomed an opportunity to discuss mutual problems and differences and called for success of the upcoming summit meeting in November between Gorbachev and President Reagan in Geneva, Switzerland.

Gorbachev and Reagan met in Geneva from November 19 to 21, 1985. Also present at the summit meeting were other high-ranking Soviet and United States officials.

A joint Soviet-American statement was issued after the summit that, in part, read as follows: "While acknowledging the differences in the sociopolitical systems of the USSR and the USA and their approaches to international issues, some greater understanding of each side's view was achieved by the two leaders. They agreed about the need to improve U.S.–Soviet relations and the international situation as a whole. In this connection the two sides have confirmed the importance of an ongoing dialogue, reflecting their strong desire to seek common ground on existing problems."

Mutual agreements that came out of the Geneva summit included the following: Both sides agreed that a nuclear war cannot be won and must never be fought. Neither side would seek to achieve military superiority over the other.

They agreed to step up their work toward negotiating on nuclear and space arms. This included the principle of reducing the nuclear arms in both countries by 50 percent. And they agreed to work toward reaching some agreement on the number and deployment of medium-range nuclear missiles in Europe.

The two leaders agreed to modernize the Soviet-United States hotline, an emergency communication system that could help prevent a nuclear war.

They also agreed to work further toward limiting the number of countries with nuclear capability. And they agreed to continue efforts toward safeguarding nuclear energy against accidents and poisoning the environment, as well as to look into more peaceful uses of nuclear energy. Both sides also said they were against chemical weapons and favored destroying existing stockpiles of such weapons.

They agreed that greater understanding was necessary between their people and encouraged greater travel and people-to-people contact. And they agreed to increase cooperation in the fields of science, education, medicine, and sports. More Soviets would learn English and more Americans would learn the Russian language.

They agreed to cooperate more on finding a cure for cancer. Finally, they agreed to encourage scientists to find ways of utilizing controlled thermonuclear fusion for peaceful purposes, to create thereby an inexhaustible source of energy for the benefit of all mankind.

Then Gorbachev and Reagan agreed to meet in the near future. (This would not happen until the Iceland summit almost a year later, in October 1986.)

Speaking to the press after the Geneva summit, Gorbachev said: "What characterizes the present stage of development of the international situation? In a nutshell, it is growing responsibility for the future of the world. The peoples have realized this tremendous responsibility, and they are doing everything they can to live up to it."[15]

He said the summit was mainly a series of private meetings he had with President Reagan. He said their discussions were straightforward, long and sharp—sometimes very sharp.

Gorbachev said he thought that improvement of Soviet-United States relations was quite possible. He said he looked to the future with optimism as he was leaving Geneva. "Common sense must prevail," he said to reporters.

His first year in office ended with an address on December 27 to the heads of various foreign diplomatic missions in the Kremlin. Gorbachev said the Soviets believed ". . . in a better future for humanity and will continue making vigorous efforts in this direction.

"There has been an exchange of signals between East and West of late, which has opened up some hope—I would put it even more cautiously, a gleam of hope—for moving forward to mutually acceptable solutions."[16]

During his first year in power, Gorbachev made an unprecedented number of changes among the men sitting in the Politburo and government. He also had set in motion a series of economic policies to cover the next fifteen years. Many social and other groups expressed hope that Gorbachev's new leadership would bring about solutions to problems that had been harming the people and the country for years and even decades.

It is believed that millions of Soviet people saw hope in their charismatic new leader and wrote to him with suggestions for projects, requests, complaints, demands for justice, appeals on behalf of friends and relatives serving prison sentences (more than two million people), and from dissidents. Gorbachev not only welcomed these letters, but began quoting from them in his speeches on national problems. So much mail of this type was written to Gorbachev that a staff of 150 people was given the job of reading and dealing with the letters.

So ended the new general secretary's first year in power. Efforts to bring about openness and change in his country were begun. And Gorbachev clearly and repeatedly voiced his hope that the nations of the world could live in peace.

It was a year of hard work with some internal opposition. But Gorbachev ended it with high hopes. He had made no major blunder. As a new world leader, he was still regarded as a friendly appearing, strong leader with a great deal of charisma. His popularity abroad was rising steadily.

The damaged area of the Chernobyl atomic plant

United States President Ronald Reagan and Soviet General Secretary Mikhail Gorbachev shake hands as they meet before their summit in Reykjavik, Iceland.

Chapter 7

CHERNOBYL AND REYKJAVIK

"It will be an important year," Gorbachev told the Communist party and the people of the Soviet Union early in 1986. "One can say [it will be] a turning point in the history of the Soviet state, the year of the Twenty-seventh Congress of the CPSU [Communist Party of the Soviet Union]. The Congress will chart the guidelines for the political, social, economic, and spiritual development of Soviet society in the period up to the next millennium. It will adopt a program for accelerating our peaceful construction.

"All efforts of the CPSU are directed toward ensuring a further improvement in the life of the Soviet people.

"A turn for the better is also needed in the international arena. This is the expectation and the demand of the peoples of the Soviet Union and of peoples throughout the world."[1]

Gorbachev said the Party's Central Committee and the Soviet government had adopted a number of foreign policy decisions.

"Our most important action is a concrete program aimed at the complete elimination of nuclear weapons throughout the world and covering a precisely defined period of time," said Gorbachev.

"The Soviet Union is proposing a step-by-step and consistent process of ridding the Earth of nuclear weapons, to be implemented and completed within the next fifteen years, before the end of the century."[2]

It was sensational news that spread across the globe. No previous Soviet leader had made such a statement or offered a program to rid the world of the nuclear threat.

Critics of President Reagan's handling of the arms race said Gorbachev scored a big psychological and public relations victory, whether the Soviet plan was genuine or could work or not.

"The twentieth century has given humanity the gift of the energy of the atom," Gorbachev said. "However, this great achievement of the human mind can turn into an instrument of the self-annihilation of the human race.

"Is it possible to solve this contradiction? We are convinced it is. Finding effective ways toward eliminating nuclear weapons is a feasible task, provided it is tackled without delay."[3]

Gorbachev said his plan for nuclear disarmament would begin that year, a year proclaimed by the United Nations to be an International Year of Peace. He recalled that the Soviet Union "was the first [nation] to raise the question of prohibiting the production and use of atomic weapons and to make atomic energy serve peaceful purposes for the benefit of humanity."[4]

Gorbachev then outlined his plan: In Stage One, within the next five to eight years, both the Soviet Union and the United States were to reduce by one-half the nuclear arms that can reach each other's territory. Each side would retain no more than six thousand warheads (missiles with nuclear capability).

In Stage Two, to start no later than 1990 and last for five to seven years, other nuclear powers also would begin to engage in nuclear disarmament. They would pledge to freeze all their nuclear arms and not have them in the other countries' territories. At the same time, the Soviet Union and the United States would continue their reduction agreements, make steps toward eliminating their medium-range nuclear weapons, and freeze their tactical nuclear systems.

After the Soviet Union and the United States would reduce their nuclear arms by 50 percent, all nuclear powers would eliminate their tactical nuclear arms. All nuclear powers also would stop nuclear-weapons tests. There also would be a ban on the development of non-nuclear weapons "based on new physical principles, whose destructive capacity is close to that of nuclear arms or other weapons of mass destruction."[5]

(This phase of Gorbachev's arms reduction plan would meet with considerable resistance from the United States because it involved limits to or halting of President Reagan's "Star Wars" defense plan. Officially called the Strategic

Defense Initiative, or SDI, the plan called for development of a sophisticated detection system above the earth that could track an enemy's missiles and shoot them down before they could hit their targets. Critics of the plan in the United States said it would cost billions of dollars and even many leading scientists doubted it ever could be invented.)

Stage Three of Gorbachev's plan, to begin no later than 1995, called for eliminating all remaining nuclear weapons. By the end of 1999, there would be no nuclear weapons left on earth. "A universal accord will be drawn up that such weapons should never again come into being,"[6] he said.

A big stumbling block in Gorbachev's arms control plan was that of verification. United States officials wondered how such a plan could be supervised so that neither side cheated on the other.

"The Soviet proposals place the USSR and the United States in an equal position," Gorbachev said. "These proposals do not attempt to outwit or outsmart the other side. We are proposing to take the road of sensible and responsible decisions."[7]

Negotiations for these plans and subsequent disarmament plans continued. On April 26, far from the Kremlin in Moscow, an event occurred that put Gorbachev on the spot for the first time in his administration. It seemed to make no difference that it was something for which he had no direct involvement.

A nuclear power plant disaster occurred in Chernobyl, a city in the Ukraine. A meltdown of the radioactive core occurred in the nuclear plant and 31 workers died. More than 200 others were treated for heavy exposure to radiation and 135,000 had to leave their homes and be relocated to other parts of the region. Radioactive clouds drifted over central Europe, Scandinavia, and then around the world, even passing over the United States.

Radiation was as high as 100,000 times normal over Poland, and 10,000 times normal in Scandinavia. Throughout Europe, crops, milk, and meat were contaminated and destroyed. Even water was radiation poisoned and great numbers of fish died.

The thousands of people evacuated from the Chernobyl area were said to be of increased risk of developing cancer in the next five to twenty years. Their health would be monitored for the rest of their lives. Also, many pregnant women from the area were told they would lose their babies and most women who might give birth later might have deformed infants.

Antinuclear demonstrations erupted around the world to protest the potential dangers from nuclear power plants everywhere. Scientists said the effects of the Chernobyl radiation would be felt for future generations, from food contamination to future cancers.

Though the disaster was blamed on operator error during

testing at the plant, Gorbachev and his administration were strongly criticized by Western officials. There had been a delay of three days before news of the meltdown had reached the West. And it came out then only because Swedish scientists questioned the unusually high radiation their instruments were recording. Gorbachev was accused of trying to keep the rest of the world from knowing about the disaster.

Gorbachev did not speak to the public about the Chernobyl accident until May 14, eighteen days after it happened. Then he was direct. He said the accident "painfully affected the Soviet people and caused anxiety among the international public."

Then he attacked Western media reports of Chernobyl and the supposed attempted cover-up as an "unrestrained anti-Soviet campaign" and an attempt to ". . . discredit the entire policy of the Soviet Union."[8] He said the Soviet Union would resume its moratorium on nuclear tests for three months and urged that the lessons of Chernobyl should speed efforts to achieve arms control.

The Chernobyl accident produced several thousand times more radioactive fallout than that measured in the World War II bombing of Hiroshima, which ushered in the Atomic Age. Yet, it produced less radioactive fallout than did the atmospheric bomb tests of the early 1960s by both the United States and the Soviet Union. However, those tests had been conducted in remote, unpopulated areas. Chernobyl, on the other hand, is only about eighty miles from Kiev, a major Soviet city of 2.5 million people.

Gorbachev did not dwell on the Chernobyl disaster when he spoke to the Soviet people about it on television. He assured them that the worst was over, then quickly changed the subject. He invited President Reagan to meet him for a new nuclear test-ban summit.

At least temporarily, Gorbachev appeared to have lost some of his charm. As Dimitri K. Simes, senior associate at the Carnegie Endowment for International Peace, said on May 14, 1986: "The Chernobyl accident was an extraordinary event. But the way it was dealt with by the Politburo was nothing but business as usual. The disillusionment with Gorbachev's charm offensive is bound to raise questions in the West as to whether it would be prudent to buy a used car from this man, or an arms control agreement, for that matter. And, as with a used car, the answer is 'yes,' provided you genuinely need it and have reliable inspection procedures. But only the incurably trusting would rely on a sweet-talking salesman's promises.

"Arms control will survive the Chernobyl disaster.

"Illusions about Mr. Gorbachev should not."[9]

Both within the Soviet Union and in other countries, many people agreed: the delay in reporting the Chernobyl disaster had dealt a severe blow to Gorbachev's campaign of "openness."

A year after the Chernobyl accident, Soviet officials said most people who lived near the plant were in good health. Three engineers at the plant went on trial charged with negligence. Soviet authorities said technical measures had been taken to improve the reliability of nuclear power stations so the accident could never occur again. The disaster cost fourteen billion dollars.

After a year, the Chernobyl disaster was not forgotten around the world, but Gorbachev's popularity seemed to have survived it. Some observers thought that was perhaps because of a slight change in Soviet thinking regarding the safety of its nuclear power plants.

An example of this was seen when Swedish officials charged that a nuclear power plant in Lithuania, another Soviet satellite, had worse safety features than Chernobyl. The Soviets shelved plans to expand the plant. It made antinuclear power critics breathe a little easier, despite the fact that there are 390 nuclear reactors known to be operating throughout the world.

In March 1987, further signs of the effects of Chernobyl within the Soviet Union were to be seen. A controversial motion picture was made by a Soviet filmmaker. *The Bells of Chernobyl*, shown first in Soviet theaters, later was shown at the Berlin International Film Festival. It was considered to be an honest, unpolitical assessment of the disaster, surprising since movies are closely controlled by the government.

The next major event in Gorbachev's second year in power came in October. He met in an agreed-upon preliminary nuclear arms race summit meeting with President Reagan. This time the meeting was held in Reykjavik, Iceland. It turned out to be one of the most promising and also controversial arms summits ever held. It also left the arms race dilemma at a deadlock in which neither side agreed to anything of substance.

The two main issues were the Antiballistic Missile (ABM) Treaty, and the United States' Strategic Defense Initiative. The ABM Treaty is an agreement between the Soviet Union and the United States on the number, size, and deployment of nuclear weapons.

Some years before, the two countries agreed to limit any defense against nuclear missile attacks by placing a small number of missiles in one location of each nation. They would be capable of intercepting and shooting down incoming nuclear missiles. A broader defense policy would be enforced, a policy called "mutual assured destruction." It meant that if one side launched a nuclear attack, the other could retaliate. This thermonuclear "tit for tat" mutual threat of destruction was believed to be a deterrent against either side striking a nuclear blow first.

So when Gorbachev and Reagan met in Reykjavik, both nations had thousands of nuclear warheads aimed at each other's country, capable of wiping out both. The Soviets had deployed a few antiballistic missiles around Moscow as the ABM Treaty permitted. The United States did not do the same in Washington, D.C., because the threat of nationwide destruction made such a limited defense seem useless.

The United States had become concerned that the Soviets were developing a nationwide nuclear defense, starting to instill a large modern radar system to guide antiballistic missiles protecting the Soviet Union. This would be in violation of the ABM Treaty. In addition, United States observers were certain that the Soviets were progressing on an SDI system of their own.

In his speech to the American people on October 14, President Reagan described his concern about keeping the Soviets within the limits of the ABM Treaty. He also reinforced his position that the United States continue research toward developing its SDI program.

"Believing that a policy of mutual destruction and slaughter of their citizens and ours was uncivilized," said Reagan, "I asked our military a few years ago to study and see if there was a practical way to destroy nuclear missiles after their launch but before they can reach their targets rather than to just destroy people. This is the goal for what we call SDI, and our scientists researching such a system are convinced it is practical and that several years down the road we can have such a system ready to deploy."[10]

It should be noted that many, including a group of the

United States' leading scientists, disagreed. They said they believed by an overwhelming margin that SDI could not produce an effective defense against a Soviet nuclear attack within the next twenty-five years. This was according to a survey conducted by Cornell University's Institute for Social and Economic Research. It was sent to 663 members of the National Academy of Sciences with expertise in physics, mathematics, and engineering.

Nonetheless, the Soviets were concerned that the United States' SDI program might give the United States an edge in nuclear defense. Some observers suggested that President Reagan use the SDI as a "bargaining chip" at the summit meeting. If he made concessions on the concept, he might win some arms reduction agreements. But Reagan refused to modify, delay, or give up the SDI program. Before the summit, Gorbachev had repeatedly said that no reductions on nuclear arms could be agreed upon if the United States insisted on preserving its SDI program. That is how Gorbachev and Reagan went into the Reykjavik summit of October 11 and 12.

On the last day of the summit, Reagan and Gorbachev met looking as if they might be close to reaching some important agreements.

The Soviets were offering drastic cutbacks on intermediate-range nuclear forces (INF). United States Secretary of State George Shultz later called the prospect "breathtaking." The cutbacks offered zero INF warheads in Europe and one hundred in Asia. To this offer, Reagan said, "Okay."

A joint working group also was making progress on issues related to nuclear testing. Its proposal called for adequate verification measures. These would be followed by reductions in either the number of tests allowed each year or the size of explosions that would be permitted. After ten years, all nuclear testing would be banned.

Reagan suggested a counterproposal in which all ballistic missiles would be eliminated during the next ten years.

Mediators for both sides suggested that within five years the number of strategic warheads on each side would be reduced from about eleven thousand to six thousand. And there would be "real limits" on heavy missiles of which the Soviets have more than the United States.

After a lengthy meeting in the morning, which ran much longer than expected, Gorbachev and Reagan took a break. During the break, Shultz and Soviet Foreign Minister Eduard Shevardnadze met with their top arms-control advisers.

One Soviet official said he felt Gorbachev had made a proposal of enormous proportion. Another claimed "a breakthrough" on arms control. He thought that after this President Reagan would go down in history as a president of peace.

It became clear that Reagan could achieve a major arms

deal, if only he would be flexible enough to make some necessary concessions on his SDI program.

Then, so close to agreement, the talks broke down. By six o'clock that Sunday night, the deadlock became evident. Reagan refused to bargain away any of his SDI program, and Gorbachev would not bargain so long as the president held to his SDI program. Gorbachev refused to accept Reagan's theory that switching from a reliance on offensive weapons to at least a partial reliance on defensive systems would add to the safety of both nations. Reagan rejected Gorbachev's argument that SDI would create a first-strike capability.

After the talks, world public opinion was divided. Almost everyone was disappointed that the two had come so close to agreement, but then had walked away from the summit with no real progress toward nuclear arms reduction.

Both sides quickly blamed the other for the failure of the talks. The two leaders left without even being able to agree on setting a date for a full-scale summit to be held sometime in the future in the United States.

Gorbachev said: "This has been a failure—and a failure when we were very close to an historic agreement."

"We came to Iceland to advance the cause of peace," said Reagan, "and though we put on the table the most far-reaching arms-control proposal in history, the general secretary rejected it."

The Soviets, Reagan said, "insisted that we sign an agreement that would deny to me and to future presidents for 10 years the right to develop, test, and deploy a defense against nuclear missiles for the people of the free world. This I could not and will not do."

Gorbachev insisted that "it would have taken a madman" to accept Reagan's position on SDI.

"The United States came to this meeting with empty hands," said Gorbachev at a news conference after the meeting. "The president of the United States did not have permission to reach agreement, and the talks collapsed."

Afterward, as both sides continued blaming the other for the deadlock, the two leaders stressed that the search for agreement would go on.

"We made great strides in Iceland," Reagan said, ". . . and we're going to continue our effort."

Gorbachev, believing that United States allies in the West might influence Reagan to make concessions on SDI in order to remove nuclear missiles aimed at them in Europe, said, "We are waiting. We are not withdrawing our proposals."[11] Maybe this influence could be put upon Reagan before upcoming nuclear arms talks in Geneva, Switzerland.

Many observers believed Reagan made a serious mistake in refusing to negotiate on SDI. He could have won so much, if he had given the Soviets some concessions on SDI. Also, most agreed that all the major concessions on arms control at the summit had come from the Soviets. They had proposed cutting the number of strategic weapons in half and reducing medium-range missiles not only in France but Asia. These arms cuts would have made the world safer.

Reagan left the summit faced with the problem of explaining why a fully developed SDI would enhance long-term prospects for peace.

On the other hand, the Soviets could expect criticism for not accepting Reagan's offer to share the benefits of SDI technology. The Soviets were doubtful such a sharing of technology could be possible.

In his television address to the Soviet people on October 14, Gorbachev said: "We were . . . literally two or three steps from making possibly historic decisions for the entire nuclear-space era, but we were unable to make those last steps. A turning point in the world's history did not take place, even though, I will say again with full confidence, it could have . . .

"We are realists and we clearly understand that the issues that have remained unsettled for many years and even decades can hardly be settled at a single sitting. We have a great deal of experience in doing business with the United States. And we are aware that the domestic political climate can change there quickly and that the opponents of peace across the ocean are strong and influencial. There is nothing new here for us.

"If we do not despair, if we do not slam the door and give vent to our emotions—although there is more than enough reason for this—it is because we are sincerely convinced that new efforts are needed aimed at building normal interstate relations in the nuclear epoch. There is no other alternative."

Chapter 8

A MAJOR ARMS REDUCTION OFFER

The Reykjavik summit talks did not sit well with many Western European leaders. They were concerned that the United States almost reached a deal with the Soviet Union to eliminate medium-range nuclear missiles from Europe. They said such an agreement might have put Western Europe at a disadvantage. If the United States withdrew its nuclear shield in Europe, the Soviets would be left with superiority in both conventional forces and shorter-range missiles.

President Reagan insisted that he agreed only to elimination of the ballistic missiles of all ranges. He would leave in place arsenals of bombers and cruise missiles.

On December 18, 1986, the Soviet Union announced it would end its unilateral ban on nuclear testing after the first American test blast of 1987. If the United States did not stop its nuclear testing, the Soviets would resume theirs.

While Soviet testing was halted "to set an example for the other nuclear powers," the United States was "stubbornly going ahead with its nuclear weapon tests,"[1] a Soviet statement said.

Early in 1987, Gorbachev turned to domestic issues and

continued his series of the most radical changes in the Soviet system since Joseph Stalin.

One proposed change was that the Soviet people be allowed to vote by secret ballot for their leaders, from the local level on up to the nation's top leaders. This was an unprecedented idea, because historically only members of the Communist party are allowed to vote. And they do not get a choice of candidates. Only one man runs for each office, and he must be a good party member. High-ranking party officials choose the candidates.

Gorbachev could not propose such a radical change in the voting system if he had not first been able to control a majority of members of the ruling Politburo. Many Soviet jobs and privileges would be in jeopardy if they came up for reelection and anyone could vote. But Gorbachev felt that the old system had to end. The old guard's grip must be broken if the Soviets were to escape from economic and political oppression and stagnation.

Gorbachev proposed the new voting system on January 29, 1987 at a meeting of the Communist Party Central Committee. He said the present system, developed under Stalin and Leonid Brezhnev, had not worked. He blamed it for national stagnation in every part of national life—political, economic, cultural, and social—and proposed to break that system.

On February 2, the United States conducted a nuclear test in violation of the existing test ban. Officials said the test was necessary to continue to verify the reliability of existing weapons and to modernize the United States nuclear arsenal. They also said the moratorium on no further testing could not be reliably verified.

On February 26, the Soviets countered with a nuclear test of their own. A nuclear device was exploded on a testing range in the remote Soviet region of Karakhstan. Soviet officials said it was their first nuclear test in more than a year and a half, since July 25, 1985.

Two days after the test, believed by some to be a domestic show of strength by Gorbachev, he appeared to back down on his strong stand against President Reagan's SDI plan and other arms control obstacles.

"The Soviet Union suggests that the problem of medium-range missiles in Europe be singled out from the package of issues [discussed at Reykjavik]," said Gorbachev, "and that a separate agreement on it be concluded without delay."[2]

The statement meant that Gorbachev was suggesting that agreement could be reached on medium-range nuclear missiles without asking for any concessions on the SDI program.

Apparently Gorbachev had decided to listen to many foreign visitors at the Kremlin-sponsored peace forum in Moscow that had taken place two weeks earlier. They had criticized him for linking his arms reduction proposals on medium-range missiles to the United States' SDI program.

Again Gorbachev had taken the initiative in appearing to

act on arms control with new and bold ideas, while President Reagan appeared only to be able to react to such proposals.

Reagan said he looked upon the new Soviet offer to separate a European middle-range nuclear missile deal from strategic arms control of SDI as a hopeful sign.

But many Europeans were still uneasy about the middle-range arms control offer. They worried now about the deployment of shorter-range Soviet missiles.

The new Gorbachev offer came at a time when President Reagan needed some good news. From late in 1986 to the time of Gorbachev's new arms control offer in the spring of 1987, Reagan and his administration were mired down in a grave scandal regarding conduct of foreign policy. A secret administration operation sold arms to Iran apparently in order to win freedom for some United States hostages.

The Iran arms sale was controversial because Reagan had repeatedly said he would never deal with terrorists. Iran is widely regarded as the seat of worldwide terrorist training and initiative. To make matters more controversial, some of the profits from the arms sales was used to supply weapons and other assistance to freedom fighters (contras) in Nicaragua.

The diversion of Iranian arms sale money to Nicaragua happened at a time when the United States Congress had passed a law forbidding such action.

Had Reagan authorized both operations? If so, his judgment in dealing with Iranian terrorists was highly criticized. But authorizing military support for the contras in Nicaragua at a time when Congress prohibited it, could put Reagan in danger of being impeached and he might be forced to resign from office.

Many wondered why Gorbachev offered to relax his stand against Reagan's SDI plan at such a crucial time in the president's term in office. Was it because Reagan needed a political lifesaver? Achieving a major agreement on arms control could win him much-needed support and a political boost.

Whatever his motives, Gorbachev gave Reagan what appeared to be a golden opportunity to regain strength and popularity, not only at home in the United States, but abroad as well. For many American and foreign observers, Gorbachev's offer seemed to be one Reagan could not refuse. The Soviet leader had made an arms reduction offer that appeared to be a giant step toward reducing the threat of nuclear war.

However, months passed and no concrete agreement was reached on Gorbachev's offer. The United States agreed only that a new arms control summit might be possible sometime in the year.

President Reagan did not jump at Gorbachev's offer. But some United States officials expressed optimism that an agreement to eliminate medium-range nuclear missiles from Europe might be complete within a few months. By late fall 1987, there could be a draft agreement from the United States that Gorbachev could consider.

On June 16, at new Geneva arms control hearings, the United States offered a new proposal of its own for the global elimination of shorter-range nuclear missiles. It also urged the Soviet Union to agree to the elimination of medium-range missiles. (The United States has no shorter-range missiles in Europe.)

On July 3, Gorbachev accused the NATO nations of hindering an agreement that could be reached by the Soviet Union and United States on medium-range missile reductions in Europe. He proposed dismantling weapons capable of mass annihilation and reducing the other weapons to a sensible level. Gorbachev said NATO was attempting to dismantle the Soviet political system and that the NATO leaders had failed to find constructive ideas on how to build East–West relations if nuclear weapons were eliminated.

Gorbachev said that despite encouraging signs, a super-power medium- and shorter-range missile pact was just a possibility due to the NATO stand.

Meanwhile, the arms negotiations continued to be deadlocked as the world was spending $900 billion a year on weapons. Continued use of billions of dollars each year on defense and arms has taken money out of many important domestic programs. Leaders of all nations taking part in the arms race realized that the money spent on defense and arms could be better used in domestic programs.

President Reagan had been strongly criticized for his insistence on high spending for defense, while the United States continued to have serious economic and social problems. Cuts in defense spending could be used to help the poor, provide money for education, modernize industry, rebuild roads and bridges, and fund many social, health, and environmental projects.

Secretary Gorbachev also saw the need for a relaxation of the arms race to use defense money for Soviet domestic programs. Many agreed it seemed wise for the two to get together and agree to an end to the expensive and potentially disastrous arms race.

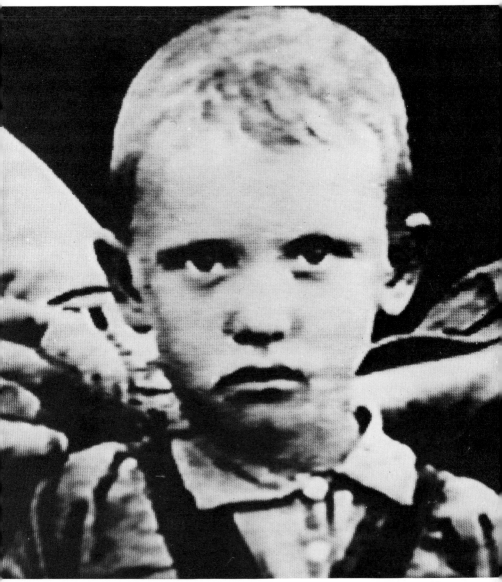

A photo of "Misha" Gorbachev taken when he was about four years old shows the effects of one of the Stalin-era famines.

The wedding portrait of Raisa and Mikhail Gorbachev taken in 1954

A 1981 photo of the CPSU Central Committee when Leonid Brezhnev was in power. Gorbachev is sixth from the right.

Three of Mikhail Gorbachev's mentors were Fyodor Kulakov (above left), Yuri Andropov (above right), and Mikhail Suslov (left).

Raisa and Mikhail Gorbachev
during an intermission at the opera
in Prague, Yugoslavia

Accompanied by his
granddaughter, Gorbachev votes as
a member of the Politburo.

The Gorbachev's daughter Irina,
granddaughter Ksenia, and son-in-
law Anatoli

On December 8, 1987, in
Washington, D.C., Gorbachev and
Reagan sign the arms reduction
treaty.

Gorbachev speaks on the 70th anniversary of the Bolshevik Revolution.

Chapter 9

A CALL FOR "RESTRUCTURING"

At a major speech to the Communist Party's Central Committee on January 28, 1987, Mikhail Gorbachev made it clear that he was in full control of the Party. He was fully determined to push through with his plans to bring about positive change, openness, and to generally "restructure" his country. Gorbachev's word for this was perestroika.

In a tough three-hour speech in Moscow, Gorbachev stressed the need to increase the democratization of Soviet society by more open election of Party officials, local representatives, and factory and collective farm administrators. He also proposed promoting qualified people to senior positions in management and other fields even if they were not members of the Party. It was a revolutionary speech because his proposals would challenge the privileges and power of not only members of the Party but the Party itself.

Gorbachev was asking for a return to what he and those supporting him in the government believed were the principles of Lenin's 1917 revolution. These included public accountability of Party organizations and popular evaluation of government and Party policies.

Gorbachev said these measures are necessary to revitalize

the country and to overcome the many problems facing the nation, including social alienation, economic stagnation, and widespread corruption.

He blamed the problems on policies and power of two of his longest-serving predecessors—Stalin and Brezhnev—who together had run the country for forty-seven years of its seventy-year history.

Among ideas Gorbachev proposed at the extraordinary meeting were: The election by secret ballot of Party chiefs from the local district to republic level. Only Party members could vote, but there would be more than one candidate for each office.

Also, "direct democracy" for the workers. They would be allowed to elect managers and executives and have a say in discussing issues such as production and personnel. This would return to Lenin's principle of "genuine self-government by the people."

Reaction, as might be expected, was not overwhelmingly in Gorbachev's favor. His reforms were going more slowly than he expected. But he insisted the reforms continued to be opposed by the older, more conservative members of the Party. Even Gorbachev admitted his reforms had the "ardent" support of the people. He also said they had the full support of the ruling Politburo.

Early in 1987, Gorbachev continued to make his political base stronger. Two close aides were promoted and one

Brezhnev appointee was dismissed from the Party leadership. At the same time, it appeared that Gorbachev could still expect to get opposition to his reforms from many of the conservatives in the Party.

A leading American expert on the Soviet Union called Gorbachev's reform campaign extraordinary, especially his bid to shake up the Soviet election system. But he warned that we would have to wait and see if Gorbachev would be around next year.

While many believed Gorbachev was approaching or at a crossroads in his political power, some Western skeptics asked if his reforms were for real or just "window dressing" for the outside world. And if his reforms were for real, would the Party and the conservative bureaucracy let him get away with them? If Gorbachev moved too fast for the Soviet army, or for Party officials, he might be removed from office before his reforms could be put in place.

Early in February 1987, Gorbachev's reform policy seemed to go another giant step further. Forty-two Soviet political dissidents were released from prisons, labor camps, or exile. They included human rights and religious activists, writers, and trade unionists.

Yelana Bonner, wife of dissident physicist Andrei Sakharov, both of whom were released from internal exile earlier in December, said that it had been a wonderful change. She also added that she hoped this was only a beginning and that all prisoners of conscience would be released soon.

At the same time, the Soviet Union began to allow more Jews to leave the country if they wished.

Gorbachev's calls for reform began showing up more openly in the Soviet press. Before Gorbachev, an editor of a newspaper or magazine did not dare to publish an article that might criticize the government or the nation's problems.

Reflecting this new openness in the public press were controversial articles in *Ogonyok*, a weekly Soviet magazine. It began publishing articles on right-wing toughs in the suburbs of Moscow and an exposé of police torture. It also published a feature to rehabilitate the reputation of a controversial poet, Nickolia Gumilyov. He had been shot in 1921 for writing poems criticizing the government. Before these articles, the magazine had mainly been bought for its crossword puzzle. Now many Soviet people couldn't find copies of the magazine, they sold so fast.

The editor, Vitaly Korotich, said his goal was simple: "To say everything that one can, while we can."

Korotich saw real progress in Gorbachev's reforms: "Up to now we've been shadowboxing over reforms. Now it's a real fight. There are real threats. Real phone calls. People call and say, 'Things will go back to the way they were, and then you'll shut up.'

"I don't think there's any alternative to what Gorbachev's doing. I know I don't want to live the old way."

Korotich put the need for reform and change in his country in an interesting way. He says that science shows how to deal with conservatives. "We are now taught that dinosaurs died out because the climate changed. So we have to change the climate."[1]

By March, Gorbachev stepped up his campaign for reform. He began making it clear that he planned a degree of structural change unprecedented in Soviet history. First calling for reform, he began to call for a revolution, not just economic change, but of political and societal "restructuring."

While few of Gorbachev's proposals had brought about any actual changes, he had succeeded in creating a new atmosphere inside the Soviet Union and a new image abroad. But observers said the real challenge to Gorbachev's ambitions and even to his survival as Soviet leader, was only beginning, as he started to carry out his policies.

As one analyst put it: "He wants to create a dynamic, technologically advanced socialist superpower, capable of competing not just militarily with the West, but economically and ideologically as well. And the emphasis is on competition, not convergence. He wants to make the Soviet Union—and with it, communism—a workable political alternative to the Western democracy."[2]

Also in March, *Pravda*, the Communist party's daily and most important newspaper, reported that abuse of power resulted in disciplinary action against 200,000 Communist party and Soviet government officials the previous year. The Soviet national prosecutor, Alexander Rekunkov, whose job is like the United States attorney general, made the announcement and complained that many other corrupt officials still remained unpunished. The officials had been found guilty of permitting the manufacture of substandard products and for breaching contracts. Most of them were fined and many lost their jobs. Under Stalin, they probably would have been exiled to Siberia or shot.

By spring of 1987, some improvement could be seen in the Soviet farm and industrial output. It was about 4 percent higher in 1986, the highest in a decade.

In April, Gorbachev found a strong friend and supporter had been elevated to more power in the government. He had known Eduard Shevardnadze when both were leaders of the Komsomol. Shevardnadze had become a strong provincial "top cop," and at about the time Gorbachev became general secretary, Shevardnadze became the Soviet foreign minister.

While Shevardnadze was considered to be a loyal Soviet leader, he also had shown he could sympathize with critics and those with little political clout. His foreign policy leadership was expected to parallel the openness and fairness Gorbachev sought in his reforms.

Still, progress on reform was not moving fast and Gorbachev still faced considerable opposition.

"It would be, at best, unrealistic to believe that such a major revolutionary turn involving the interests of millions and millions of people and our entire society is proceeding easily," Gorbachev said in May. "I want to emphasize the reorganization is a long and difficult process."

Speaking to Soviet editors, radio, and TV newsmen, Gorbachev said: "Apparently some people would very much like to convince their readers and listeners that the Soviet Union has at last embarked on the type of democracy existing in the West. Things stand, I would say, quite the opposite."[3]

Gorbachev said his reforms represent the essence of Communist dogma as laid down by Lenin and will result in "Socialist democracy."

At this time Gorbachev allowed a small hint into his personal life. He said his greatest weakness was that he was interested in too many issues across too many fields of endeavor. For example, he said he had entered Moscow State University intending to study physics but graduated from the law faculty. He also said the responsibilities of his job left him with little free time for pursuing such personal interests as history and literature.

On May 20, 1987, Gorbachev said he still thought an agreement on medium-range nuclear missiles in Europe was possible. But he expressed dismay at what he described as the growing number of conditions placed on a possible treaty by the United States and its allies.

Gorbachev said he would accept a NATO demand for the elimination of all Soviet SS-20 medium-range missiles worldwide, but only if the United States removed its nuclear weapons from Japan, South Korea, and the Philippines.

Gorbachev suffered something of a political black eye early in March. Reports circulated that a videotape was being passed around Moscow showing his wife, Raisa, to be an extravagant, vain woman. It showed her shopping in exclusive Paris dress shops and using an American Express credit card to buy jewelry in London.

Raisa, an attractive and well-dressed woman, had received considerable attention from the world press during the summit meeting and other trips abroad with her husband. But even United States observers conceded that the videotape might only have been part of an internal campaign to discredit Gorbachev and thereby try to undermine his authority.

At this time, former United States Secretary of State Henry Kissinger said that because of Gorbachev's political problems, he gave him more than a fifty-fifty chance of remaining in power for more than five years.

On April 16, Gorbachev acknowledged for the first time that his plans to restructure Soviet society were resisted by officials as highly placed as the three-hundred-member Council Committee that sets Communist party policy.

In a televised ninety-minute speech to a congress of the

Young Communist League, Gorbachev said he has been asked in letters to identify opponents of his policies.

"We don't have political opponents, no opposition to restructuring," he said. "[But] the difficulty of the beginning steps of these revolutionary changes does exist."

He said those who were trying to slow down the changes were in the Central Committee and the government, in the ministries, republics, and provinces. "They exist in the work collectives and even in the Komsomol."[4]

That same month, Andrei Sakharov, the Soviet physicist and human-rights activist who had been released from exile, said he supported Gorbachev's reform efforts: "Regarding human rights, the West must keep pressure on the Soviet Union for everyone's sake. The issues of prisoners of conscience and emigration complicate Gorbachev's reform efforts. He really wants to dispose of the problem, but his comrades won't support him. To continue the pressure from the West will help Gorbachev, give him leverage with others in the leadership. This is a great help to him, really, as it was to me.

"There is no turning back from glasnost, the new policy of openness," said Sakharov. "But it is just a start."[5]

Gorbachev agreed, in his January 1987 speech to the Communist Party Central Committee on reorganizing and the Party's personnel policy: "We are just getting into stride, finding concrete approaches in our political line and mapping out ways of attaining the targets we have set ourselves. We are just turning on the mechanism and means of reorganization and making our first steps in having them swing into action and yield results. But already today as we reviewed the results of 1986, we saw that headway had been made.

"How has progress been made? It is the direct result of our people's support for the line towards reorganization, towards acceleration.

"The cause of reorganization, the cause of the revolutionary revitalization of society, and the country's future are in the hands of the people. The future will be what we make it, by our common labour, our intellect, and our conscience.

"We are firm in our desire to carry out the decisions of the 27th Congress. We shall press on with bringing Soviet society to a qualitatively new peak in life. We are confident that reorganization is irreversible."

Chapter 10

THE BEGINNING OF CHANGE

While America's impressions of Gorbachev were generally favorable and hopeful, an incident occurred in September 1986 that made them wonder. An American correspondent, Nicholas Daniloff, had been arrested in Moscow and was accused of being a spy. Some observers wondered if Gorbachev was responsible and ordered Daniloff held as a hostage in trade for a Soviet man being held on spy charges in the United States.

Shortly after, both supposed spies were exchanged and the incident ended almost as fast as it began. It was not possible to tell if Gorbachev knew about the Daniloff arrest or was behind any effort to have the Soviet man released by trading Daniloff for him.

In February 1987, the Soviet Union invited a rather odd assortment of American and foreign celebrities to attend its peace conference in Moscow. It was not certain whether Gorbachev had drawn up the guest list, which included respected British novelist Graham Greene, American writer Norman Mailer, and entertainers Kris Kristofferson, Yoko Ono, Paul Newman, and Gregory Peck.

At the same time, some American journalists wondered

why Gorbachev needed to win over such celebrities. They reported public opinion polls that indicated Gorbachev was already more trusted on arms control by the West European public than was President Reagan. And they believed Gorbachev was on his way to achieving the same place in American public opinion polls.

They thought his peace congress might take him closer to that goal. At the peace congress, Gorbachev stressed that his dramatic reform policies were of more immediate importance than were his foreign policies. Even so, he made further peace offers by proposing the elimination of "all" foreign military bases.

"I state with full responsibility," Gorbachev said, "that our international policy is more than ever determined by domestic policy, by our own interest in concentrating on constructive endeavors to improve our country. . . . This is where we want to direct our resources."

Gorbachev proposed the removal of all military bases on foreign soil. It was another major peace proposal such as Gorbachev's surprising and far-reaching proposal at Reykjavik to eliminate "all" nuclear weapons by the end of the century. "All" would have to include Soviet military bases in the satellite countries such as Poland, Czechoslovakia, and Hungary as well as in East Germany and Afghanistan.

One United States political observer said that Soviet military withdrawal from those countries would be the most significant change in international affairs since the close of World War II.

Some accused Gorbachev of not meaning what he said, and merely practicing propaganda. But in any case, President Reagan did not pick up on Gorbachev's broad-ranging proposal. It was at a time when Reagan and his administration had become more occupied by the scandal of arms sales to Iran and diversion of some resulting funds to supply the resistance fighters in Nicaragua.

Shortly after the Soviet peace congress, former Secretary of State Henry Kissinger and several other American diplomats met with Gorbachev in Moscow, late in February 1987. It had been about two years since Gorbachev had first spoken of the need for reform, and Kissinger saw little if any change. In fact, Kissinger said he still found an atmosphere in Moscow of "ambivalence." And he found the Soviet capital to be just as "seedy" and "backward" as ten years before.

"One remains amazed that a country subsisting at so marginal a standard of living should conduct so assertive a global policy," Kissinger noted.

Yet, Kissinger thought the "surface impression of stagnation was misleading. There is clearly an unprecedented ferment underneath the gloomy surface of wintry Moscow. The new leadership [under Gorbachev] is different. It displays a vigor, dynamism and flexibility inconceivable 10 years ago."

Kissinger said he found Gorbachev's predecessor, Brezhnev, to be "ebullient" but slightly insecure in dealing with Americans, spoke from prepared statements, and relied heavily on his associates.

"Mikhail Gorbachev and his colleagues are far more urbane," Kissinger said. Gorbachev spoke off the cuff for several hours, then later from a prepared statement.

Kissinger found Gorbachev to be a forceful personality, but did not think that was entirely a blessing for the United States.

Gorbachev said that Soviet-United States relations were at a crossroads. Kissinger agreed and afterward said he favored continuing consultation with Gorbachev and stated several conclusions: "'Reform' is in the air. I do not doubt the sincerity of the effort to overcome the stagnation, technological backwardness and corruption of traditional Soviet-style central planning.

"The purpose of that reform is not to spur democracy or freedom; it is to encourage efficiency and industrial progress, hence to make the Soviet Union more powerful."[1]

Zbigniew Brzezinski, national security adviser when Jimmy Carter was president of the United States, wondered if President Reagan was ready or able to grasp the opportunities Gorbachev might present.

Reagan had formed his foreign policy beliefs based on Soviet leaders and events during the Cold War era after

World War II. He came to office in 1981 confident he knew what to expect from the "old men" who then ruled the Soviet Union.

A pattern definitely had been set, since aged, ailing Kremlin leaders such as Leonid Brezhnev, Yuri Andropov, and Konstantin Chernenko appeared to symbolize the failure of Soviet communism. Reagan had called it a system that one day would be relegated to "the ash heap of history."

During the first four years of his presidency, Reagan had dealt with three of those sick old men in the Kremlin. But things changed when Gorbachev became general secretary. It did not take Gorbachev long before he began talking of major reforms and changes that would pull the Soviet Union out of its stagnant, corrupt past and put it on a new course of productivity and openness.

Gorbachev's suggestions for arms reduction and elimination of military bases were bolder than any Reagan offered. Gorbachev appeared to be winning at least a public relations battle with Reagan.

"A skillful public relations effort has become an important component of Moscow's diplomacy," said Dimitri K. Simes, senior associate at the Carnegie Endowment for International Peace, writing in *Foreign Affairs* magazine. "But the substance of the U.S.S.R.'s international behavior also has changed considerably."

Simes said the new team Gorbachev brought into the

government with him not only has launched Gorbachev's "charm offensive" toward the West, but also introduced a wide variety of foreign policy initiatives.

One American correspondent in Moscow said, "Now it is President Reagan who is the old man in the superpower rivalry [Reagan was seventy-five in 1987] struggling to match adroit propaganda thrusts by the 56-year-old general secretary . . ."

However, criticism of Gorbachev's programs for change and reform continued within the Soviet Union and by spring of 1987 appeared to be resisted by all strata of society. The criticism began to take on all the signs of a struggle over the Soviet Union's character as the Party began preparing for the November 7, 1987, 70th anniversary of the 1917 revolution. Which, if any, side would win? Gorbachev and his reformers, or their conservative rivals?

Gorbachev's exhausting schedule of speeches and meetings to keep his reform program going was causing him to draw heavily on his vitality and intellect as well as his comparative youth. Maybe too, Gorbachev had time on his side. The old conservative guard in the Kremlin couldn't live forever.

From all of this one thing was apparent. Gorbachev was a fighter. He was working harder than perhaps any national leader in the world to bring about positive change for his country and his people, at the risk of his own political future.

And he appeared to be working equally as hard on arms reduction and world peace.

In the spring of 1987, Gorbachev visited many of the Soviet Union's satellite countries. He received generally strong welcomes in Czechoslovakia, Romania, Hungary, Poland, and other countries. He encouraged them to look to their own reforms and openness.

Gorbachev also met with Great Britain's Prime Minister Margaret Thatcher and reaffirmed his commitment to sweeping reforms in his country. He began exploring diplomatic exchanges with Israel, a country the Soviet Union had been at odds with for years, and hinted at allowing thousands of Soviet Jews to be permitted to leave the country if they wished.

Meanwhile, the United States and its allies continued to wonder what a reformed Soviet Union and a stronger general secretary would mean for them. No Western leader was as yet publicly saying they wished Gorbachev well. But some United States-Soviet analysts believed the United States could gain from Gorbachev succeeding in his reforms.

"Should Gorbachev prevail, do his policies bode fair or ill for the West?" asked Walter C. Clemens, Jr., professor of political science at Boston University and a research fellow at Harvard University's Center for Science and International Affairs. "Basic Western interests would not suffer if the USSR liberalized economically and the system yielded greater abundance. True, more resources could then go to arms, but history shows that rising living standards generate powerful demands for ever more creature comforts. And Soviet society lacks any strong constituency for foreign adventure or confrontation."[2]

While Western diplomats and analysts continued to consider the effects Gorbachev's reforms would have on the United States and its allies, a lucky break literally flew out of the skies of Moscow for Gorbachev.

A teenage West German pilot flew his single-engine Cessna Skyhawk plane from Finland on May 28, 1987, landing it right in the heart of Red Square at 7:30 in the evening. It happened, by coincidence, while Soviet soldiers were celebrating National Border Guard Day.

Somehow, nineteen-year-old Matthias Rust managed to enter Soviet airspace without being detected. He circled above Red Square three times, buzzed the Lenin Mausoleum, then landed, and stopped his plane just a few yards away from the Kremlin wall.

Rust stepped from the cockpit and found himself surrounded by crowds of Soviet citizens amazed at seeing him land his plane in such a secret and well-guarded zone. He managed to sign a few autographs before Soviet militiamen arrested him. As he was being led away, one official remarked, "Just put this down as another example of our new openness."[3]

The unauthorized flight and landing in Red Square resulted in the sacking of Air Defense Commander Aleksandr Koldunov and gave Gorbachev an unexpected opportunity to shake up the military. It had been Gorbachev's contention for some time that the first step toward achieving a more reliable defense system for the Soviet Union was to achieve better management, not spend more millions of dollars on better military and defense equipment.

The West German teenager said he had only flown over Moscow and landed in Red Square on a lark, but he was to be tried anyway. Violating Soviet territory carries a penalty of up to ten years in prison. Rust was given four years, but was freed in August 1988.

What the incident did was to allow Gorbachev to call for a major overhaul of the Soviet armed forces. And it reminded Western observers that there could be sternness behind Gorbachev's smile. Gorbachev could act decisively and perhaps brutally, if the situation required. This time he was going to bite down hard on one of the major institutions of Soviet power needing reform, the Soviet armed forces.

Shortly after, Gorbachev began firing and promoting military brass. Out went seventy-nine-year-old Defense Minister Sergei Sokolov for an early retirement. Koldunov lost his job as commander of air defense for "negligence and lack of organization." Gorbachev replaced them with younger men of lesser experience whom he could easily control.

Some observers now saw evidence that Gorbachev was nearer to consolidating his power.

"This affair puts to rest stories about Gorbachev's lack of control in the Politburo," said Dimitri K. Simes. "We are talking about a very powerful chief executive and commander in chief."[4]

By the summer of 1987, Soviet citizens were still carrying their "maybe bags," looking for a line to stand in to buy anything, because they needed everything. And what few worthwhile consumer goods were available cost a lot of money. A video recorder, if one could be found to buy in the Soviet Union, cost about the equivalent of $2,600 or half a year's wages.

But glasnost was to be seen in some unexpected places. The new openness even extended to relaxing a ban on rock music. Soviet youth have formed rock bands imitating Western music and performance styles and are starting to stomp and scream in concerts performed by their own rock stars. They seem to be able to play whatever they want.

As part of a cultural exchange, Soviet humorists traveled to the United States to study what makes Americans laugh. They came to the conclusion that Americans giggle too much. One said they had never considered America to be a nation of gloomy people. But after their visit, they thought maybe Americans smiled and laughed and giggled perhaps too much.

Anything can be funny to an American, the Soviet humorists were shocked to find. Americans laugh at jokes about handicapped people and even about AIDS.

In 1988, a United States delegation went to the Soviet Union to find out what makes Russians laugh. They discovered Soviets under Gorbachev *do* have a sense of humor. A Moscow rock critic, analyzing the new freedom for pop singers under glasnost, said that there were no limits on songs about social problems, some limits on political songs, but there was still no mention of sex.

One Soviet poet likened Gorbachev's call for glasnost to a war. He said it was similar to the Bolsheviks, seizing power nearly seventy years ago.

But traditionally, the Russian people are slow to change and skeptical about change. Gorbachev still had powerful critics in the Communist party. Whether he succeeds or not might depend on whether the people want reforms and change. If the people do not show their leaders they want reform, they will not get it and Gorbachev could be removed from power.

Gorbachev had to reach not only the bureaucracy but the people to gain support for his reforms. In January 1987, he spoke to the Communist Party Central Committee: "How has progress been made? It is the direct result of our people's support for the line towards reorganization, towards acceleration.

"How can we fail to see this or say that nothing has happened or nothing is taking place? The revolutionary is not the one who uses revolutionary phrases, but the one who can view things in perspective and rouse the people and the Party to protracted and persistent effort, taking note of every step of progress and using it to find another fulcrum for a new and broader stride.

"We need democracy—like air. If we fail to realize this or if we do realize it and draw no real serious steps to broaden it, to promote it and draw the country's working people extensively into the reorganization process, our policy will get choked, and reorganization will fail . . ."

Gorbachev said the Communist party is firmly of the opinion that the people should know everything.

"Openness, criticism and self-criticism, and control exercised by the masses are guarantees for Soviet society's healthy development. Since the people need them, this means that they are really needed.

"In our state, a state of workers and peasants, everything concerns the people, because it is a state of the people. They should know everything and be able to consciously judge everything. These words, as you know, were said by Lenin.

"Openness, criticism, and self-criticism are vital for us. These are major requisites of the socialist way of life. . . . [They] are necessary for our advance, for accomplishing immense tasks.

"The people will judge our policy and our efforts of reorganization and they will do this ever more strictly, by the tangible results we achieve in securing real improvements in the working and living conditions of the millions.

"Reorganization is the frontline for every honest person, for every patriot. There is enough work for everyone and the road ahead is long.

"We shall press on with bringing Soviet society to a qualitatively new peak in life. We are confident that reorganization is irreversible."

Gorbachev spoke as passionately and eloquently for world peace in March 1987, when he addressed a forum in Moscow "For a Nuclear-Free World, for the Survival of Humanity."

"At our meeting in Geneva, the US President said that if the earth faced an invasion by extraterrestrials, the US and the Soviet Union would join forces to repel such an invasion. I shall not dispute the hypothesis, though I think it's early yet to worry about such an intrusion. It is more important to realize the need to eliminate the nuclear threat and accept that there is no roof on earth or in space to save us if a nuclear storm broke out.

"Our idea of creating a comprehensive system of international security and our other initiatives clearly show that the Soviet Union is willing and ready to renounce its nuclear power status and reduce all other armaments to a bare essential. Look at all our proposals. They don't mean leaving any of our weapons outside negotiation. Our principle is simple: All weapons must be limited and reduced, and those of wholesale annihilation eventually scrapped.

"The historic goal before us, that of a demilitarized world, will have to be achieved stage by stage, of course. In each phase, there must definitely be respect for mutual interests and a balance of reasonable sufficiency constantly declining. Everybody must realize and agree: Parity in the potential to destroy one another several times over is madness and absurdity. Humanity must get stronger and enter the post-nuclear age.

"Is that possible? Some believe it is, others think not. No use arguing about it now. I think life will have its way. By and large, the peoples are coming to realize that. They already realize that a nuclear war must never be fought. So let us take the first big step: Cut the nuclear arsenals and keep space weapon-free. Let us start from the vantage point of Reykjavik, and then move on and see how that will affect the international atmosphere. My own feeling is that each such step will make for greater confidence and open fresh vistas for cooperation. And more democratic thinking at the international level, equality, and the independent and active participation of all nations—large, medium, and small—in the affairs of the world community must help the process."

Chapter 11

A THAW IN THE COLD WAR

Was he sick? Was he deposed? Where *was* he?

In the late summer of 1987, Mikhail Gorbachev vanished. After a public appearance on August 7, he dropped from sight for almost seven weeks.

Speculation began to spread that he was ill, or maybe he was involved in a political power struggle to keep from being ousted as general secretary. Had he gone too far with his reform programs and did top party officials want his head?

Gorbachev put an end to the rumors, all wrong, when he surprised everyone by reappearing in public on September 29. He explained he had merely taken a vacation, but would not say where he and his wife, Raisa, had gone. Some reports said they went to Yalta, a southern resort.

Gorbachev had worked on his vacation. He spent some of the time writing a speech for the upcoming 70th anniversary of the Bolshevik Revolution and putting finishing touches on a new book. But looking tanned and relaxed, it was obvious Gorbachev had benefitted from his fifty-two-day absence, one of the most private escapes from public view of a powerful head of state in modern memory.

Gorbachev's new book *Perestroika, New Thinking for Our Country and the World*, attracted worldwide attention upon its publication that November. It set forth his plans and hopes for restructuring his country, largely based on his blueprint for improving Soviet life by revamping and reenergizing the nation's sagging economy.

The word perestroika now became a rallying cry, a catchword for all his reforms. It was intended to spark a new idealism and patriotism, as well as a sense of new hope, in his people.

Gorbachev conceded in his book that his call for reforms, for openness and change, depended on the people wanting and accepting them. In his book he wrote, "In the final account, the most important thing for the success of perestroika is the people's attitude to it.

"Perestroika means mass initiative . . . the initial task of restructuring—an indispensable condition necessary if it is to be successful—is to 'wake up' those people who have 'fallen asleep' and make them truly active and concerned, to ensure that everyone feels as if he is the master of the country, of his enterprise, office or institute.

"This is the main thing. To get the individual involved in all processes is the most important aspect of what we are doing."[1]

Gorbachev faced not only skepticism or even downright fear of reform from some of the population, but also from some of the Kremlin's other leaders. Viktor Chebrikov, head of the KGB, the powerful Soviet secret police, and Yegor Ligachev, the second-ranking Soviet leader after Gorbachev, and some leaders of the armed forces all voiced concerns about the general secretary's reform programs. Not only the extent, but the speed of the changes worried them.

Perhaps because of this opposition or skepticism, Gorbachev appeared to agree to a slowing down of his reform programs. This position seemed to align him with centrists in the party demanding a slower pace to restructuring.

But Gorbachev may only have given into them temporarily, using political strategy, to gain more support in his country before joining President Reagan at a summit in Washington that December.

At the forefront of Gorbachev's plans for economic reform and growth for his country was a need to get an arms reduction agreement with Reagan. The money spent on the arms race could be put to better use getting the Soviet Union on stronger economic feet.

In November, Gorbachev had to eat political pie, as many leaders often have to. One of his comrades and protégés, a strong supporter of perestroika, Moscow Communist Party Chief Boris N. Yeltsin, was accused of disloyalty and "grave party crimes." It was little more than a throwback to the Stalin-era's political witch-hunts, but Yeltsin had lost favor in the party. Gorbachev might have saved his friend his job, but apparently out of political expediency, he did not oppose conservatives who wanted Yeltsin out. They felt threatened because he had been urging Gorbachev to implement his reforms faster. Later Yeltsin was given another, less important job.

Was Gorbachev the crusader caving in to his opponents and critics? Probably not. He was just doing what most other heads of state sometimes must do. He was playing politics, to give a little now in order to gain more later.

In December, a Soviet filmmaker, Tengiz Abuldaze, attacked the bureaucrats, the high-level executives in government and industry and on the farms. There were eighteen million of them, about half the nation's population, and he said their numbers should be reduced by two-thirds. "These people will be the most terrible enemies of the perestroika," he said, because they would resist change since it could mean they would lose their jobs or power.

Another intellectual, novelist Vasil Bykov, said the "overwhelming majority" of people thirst for reform "because they see the only way out of economic and general stagnation in the radical restructuring of our entire life . . ."[2]

Reforms, meanwhile, continued. The Soviet criminal code was rewritten, calling for an end to the punishment of internal exile for political dissidents who were sent to labor camps or prison for writing or speaking out against the government. Shorter prison terms also would be given for some political crimes, reduced from fifteen to ten years.

A strong, confident Gorbachev addressed the Communist party leaders at the opening of festivities that November marking the 70th anniversary of the Bolshevik Revolution. But politician Gorbachev took control over reformer Gorbachev and he tempered his words about change. He stuck more to national history than his program for perestroika, apparently to appease conservatives still opposed to his reforms.

But he did say that his program of restructuring was the most important step taken by the Soviet Union since the revolution.

Also in his speech, Gorbachev urged new, more relaxed relationships with other Communist countries. He said that no longer would the Kremlin dictate strict policy to its allies. It was another major reform and a significant break with previous Soviet policy. He urged a more sophisticated culture of mutual relations among progressive forces that would take into account the diversity of the Soviet allies.

In the weeks before the December summit in Washington, D.C., Gorbachev and Reagan had another go-around about SDI. Gorbachev insisted he would not bargain on nuclear arms reductions unless Reagan gave up his Strategic Defense Initiative program. As before, Reagan refused to bargain away his pet defense program.

Then, when it looked as if the summit would not take

place, Gorbachev appeared to back down. He seemed to have changed his mind and was now willing to meet with Reagan to sign an arms reduction pact even if differences remained over SDI.

An American air force general, John Piotrowski, reported at this time that the Soviets had developed lasers powerful enough to destroy low-orbiting United States satellites and damage those farther away. Maybe Gorbachev was no longer so worried about the SDI program because his country's own antimissile defense program was already in place.

Reagan, meanwhile, pressed Gorbachev to make reforms in human rights, for political dissidents, Soviet Jews wanting to leave the country, and for those persecuted in Soviet satellite nations. Gorbachev agreed that a discussion of human rights could be put on the summit agenda.

Summit fever began to spread over Washington. United States families from across the nation began inviting Gorbachev and Raisa to visit them on their stay in America. Some even sent their house keys.

Congressional leaders considered inviting Gorbachev to address a joint meeting of the House and Senate. But a furor broke out, since this was an honor normally reserved only for leaders of America's allies. Despite Gorbachev's overtures of friendship and peace, the United States still considered the Soviet Union a hostile country and a foe of human rights. A conservative Republican protest led to the cancellation of any offer for Gorbachev to address Congress.

On December 1, Gorbachev confirmed that the Soviet Union was conducting research on its own version of an SDI missile defense. But he again urged Reagan to abandon his SDI program or there would be no agreement on arms reduction. He said that if that happened, Reagan would be blamed for renewing the arms race.

But despite the SDI disagreement, negotiators for the Soviets and the United States worked up an historic arms reduction treaty. Gorbachev and Reagan would sign it at their summit meeting in Washington. It would eliminate intermediate-range nuclear weapons, an entire class of nuclear missiles then being deployed by both countries and their allies in Europe and Asia. Hopes also were held out that another agreement could be reached to cut long-range missiles by 50 percent.

On the first day of the summit, December 8, 1987, Gorbachev and Reagan signed the unprecedented nuclear arms reduction treaty by which the United States and Soviets would destroy all their medium-range nuclear missiles, numbering about twenty-six hundred. They also agreed to destroy thirty-two nuclear warheads within three years.

The old stumbling block to arms reduction was verification. Both sides agreed to strict rules by which on-site inspection could be made to verify that each country's missiles were in fact being destroyed.

But while peace seekers around the world sighed some relief in the elimination of the medium-range missiles, others still worried. The missiles to be destroyed represented only 3 percent of the Soviet Union's and the United States' nuclear arsenals. Still, most agreed the treaty was an important step toward global peace.

The treaty had to be ratified, by the Soviet Parliament and the United States Senate. There was little doubt the Supreme Soviet would ratify the treaty almost immediately, since Gorbachev had its support in the arms reduction offer. But in the United States Senate, there were those who opposed the treaty, either for political reasons or for fear that verification would not be possible.

After dealing with arms control, Gorbachev and Reagan discussed human rights and other issues. Reagan pressed for the right of Soviet Jews to leave the Soviet Union if they chose. He also asked that the Soviets get their troops out of Afghanistan, which had been invaded nearly ten years previously, and to stop interfering in Africa and Central and South America. Gorbachev tied withdrawal of Soviet troops from Afghanistan to a demand that the United States first cut off aid to Afghan rebels fighting the Soviets there.

Despite no gains on human rights or most other issues, the Washington summit was considered a success. Both leaders left the door open for another summit, to be held in Moscow. Maybe the arms reduction treaty could be ratified by then.

Later it was revealed that Gorbachev had talked to Reagan during the summit and offered to cut off military aid to Nicaragua in return for an end to the United States aid to the contras there. But Reagan did not pick up on the offer and nothing came of it. Analysts concluded it was because aid to the contras, rebels fighting the leftist Sandanista regime in Nicaragua, was one of Reagan's favorite causes. He did not want to agree to anything that would keep him from continuing to aid the rebels.

Shortly before the year ended, Mikhail Gorbachev's portrait graced the cover of *Time* magazine in America and its editors named him the "Man of the Year." Making *Time*'s cover and getting that title confirmed what many around the world had thought: Gorbachev's reform efforts and his initiatives toward arms reduction had earned him high marks as a world leader working for peace—apparently higher than Reagan's.

(Six months later, on June 6, 1988, Raisa's portrait would be on the cover of *Time*, symbolizing hope for Soviet women to gain their own reforms in a male-dominated country.)

On New Year's Eve, Gorbachev talked to the people over television. He promised more progress in arms control and that "immense and hard work" was ahead in his drive for economic change.

Gorbachev started the new year of 1988 with a major reform. He announced that Soviet companies would henceforth have to show a profit or suffer government penalties that could lead to eventual closing. It was a first step in his plan to shake the nation's industries out of the old system of a central bureaucracy. He encouraged local managers to take more control and implement capitalist factors such as profit motive, supply and demand, and individual initiative.

Early in January, steps were taken to reform the electoral process in the country. It was reported that instead of the Communist party assigning only one candidate for each office, multiple candidates might be allowed to run for the Supreme Soviet. But even if this reform went into effect, it would not mean much, since candidates would still be hand-picked by the Party, not the people.

Still, Gorbachev vowed that his reform could turn the Soviet Union into the world's most "democratic" country. He did not mean it would be a democracy like the United States. But the Soviet Union would be a more just country, recognizing the rights and freedoms of the people and giving them more of a say in their own government. He would just take some of the things from Western democracy that might be good for his country, such as some of the capitalist philosophies, to strengthen the Soviet economy and make the country work better.

But to make the country work better would mean that perhaps millions would lose their jobs. The Communist party newspaper *Pravda* said that about sixteen million

Soviets would be laid off in the next twelve years because of campaigns for job efficiency and discipline. It was a frightening report to many, since Soviet citizens are guaranteed jobs by their constitution. There is no such thing in the Soviet Union as unemployment. Everyone works, goes to school, or is in the armed forces. They may not like the job they are assigned to, but they have a job.

Gorbachev assured the people that job placement centers would be created to provide retraining and occupational counseling for those laid off. New jobs would be found for them in the more efficient new labor system.

In February, East German news reports revealed that the Soviets had begun dismantling part of their intermediate-range nuclear arsenal in that satellite country. This was done even before the United States Senate ratified the arms control treaty in an apparent attempt to show Soviet willingness to comply with verification rules.

In April, the Soviets agreed to pull their troops out of Afghanistan, which they had invaded in 1979. It had been a futile war for years because of strong Afghan guerrilla resistance and had cost thousands of Soviet lives and a great deal of money. Some 115,000 Soviet troops would be withdrawn from Afghanistan over a nine-month period.

Apparently the Soviets decided it was a no-win war, such as the United States had fought in Vietnam. It was time to give it up and bring an end to the loss of life and the waste of money, money that could be better spent in Soviet domestic programs. Pulling out of Afghanistan also gave Gorbachev a good bargaining chip to use in future arms control dealings with Reagan, since that had been one of Reagan's preconditions for negotiating.

Also in April, reform reached the farms of the Soviet Union. The Politburo announced that agricultural cooperatives would henceforth be put on an equal footing with collective and state farms begun under Stalin in the 1930s. Unlike collective and state farms, cooperatives have greater say in what they grow and are allowed a share of the profits. The new status was in keeping with Gorbachev's promise of bringing democracy to the cooperative farmers. More freedom to run a farm would, it was hoped, result in greater production. Then the Soviets would not have to pay so much to import grain and other food from the United States and other countries.

As reform continued, by May concern began growing among intellectuals supporting perestroika. It was reported that many Soviet intellectuals now openly debated whether Gorbachev was risking being overthrown by pressing for more change and reform. They expressed concern that it had happened before and could again. Former Kremlin leader Nikita Khrushchev had been removed from power in 1964 when opponents thought he had gone too far in asking for reforms.

Adding fuel to the fears of reformers, Soviet militiamen broke up a conference by political activists trying to organize a party in opposition to the ruling Communist party. Five persons were arrested and others were detained and questioned about attempting to form a democratic union, which would be an alternative to the Communist party.

Despite the outcome of this attempt to challenge the power of the party leaders, it was remarkable that such an attempt would have been made at all. Before Gorbachev and glasnost, such a meeting would never have taken place, or its organizers would have been shot or put in prison.

That May, Gorbachev had to admit that reform was not going smoothly, after assessing progress in many areas.

He said he had found confusion in the minds of many people, workers, intellectuals, and administrators, not only at the ground level, but on the top also.

He urged the editors to give perestroika a second chance.

At about this time, some reform-minded party officials began considering the possibility of setting age limits and fixing the terms of office for the country's leaders. Some even suggested that the general secretary no longer be a lifelong position, but be limited to two or three terms of eight years each.

Gorbachev had recommended a new system to replace older officials in top party jobs about a year before, to breathe younger life into the government run by men mostly in their seventies and eighties. Now party leaders appeared to be willing to consider even this reform. It probably would not apply to those already holding office, but to those who would come after the present older regime retired or died in office.

Gorbachev's plea the previous November for more independence for the Soviet satellite countries bore fruit in March. He made a five-day state visit to Yugoslavia and a joint Soviet-Yugoslav declaration resulted. It said the two nations were proceeding from the conviction that no one had a monopoly over the truth and that Communist leaders of the two nations have no pretensions of imposing their concepts of social development on anyone.

The Soviets, in a major move to signal a loosening of their grip on Eastern bloc states, agreed to a new policy allowing other Communist states the inalienable right to decide independently their own roads of social development.

Also in March, negotiations began for another summit between Gorbachev and Reagan, to be held this time in Moscow. But delays in the United States Senate to ratify the medium-range nuclear missile treaty made it doubtful an additional arms reduction agreement could be reached at the summit. Opposition to the agreement still centered mainly on the realities of verification.

Reagan agreed to go to Moscow to show a further willingness to negotiate with Gorbachev on arms control and other issues. He made it clear that another subject he was eager to discuss with Gorbachev was human rights.

Gorbachev's campaign for reform passed an important test on May 23, when the party's Central Committee endorsed a blueprint for reforms to be debated at a conference the following month. Committee leaders approved ideas for restructuring society submitted by the Politburo. They agreed to a platform allowing the party to "forge ahead." It was considered a victory for Gorbachev and perestroika.

Then, just as it looked as if the United States Senate would not ratify the arms reduction treaty, skepticism of verification seemed to fade away and disputes over the treaty were suddenly resolved. United States Secretary of State George Shultz met with Soviet Prime Minister Eduard Shevardnadze for two days. Then the two reached an agreement on verification that apparently appeased some reluctant United States senators.

On May 27, the Senate voted 93-5 to approve the Intermediate-range Nuclear Forces Treaty, the first arms control agreement to eliminate an entire class of nuclear weapons.

Reagan and his wife, Nancy, went to Moscow and at the opening of the five-day summit on May 29, Reagan challenged Gorbachev to do more on human rights for Soviet Jews and dissidents. Gorbachev took offense and cautioned Reagan that he did not need a lecture on how to govern his people.

But Reagan persisted and, in between conferences with Gorbachev, met with Soviet dissidents and listened to their complaints. He spoke little in public about arms control and kept hammering away on human rights.

Gorbachev dealt with this pressure as diplomatically as he could. Finally, perhaps convincing him that Reagan did not know of the advances that had been made in human rights in the Soviet Union, Reagan appeared suddenly to switch his position. Before the summit ended, Reagan gave a surprising speech. He said he was sure that human rights violations in the Soviet Union were not a result of government policy but merely a misfortune due to bureaucracy. Such a reversal angered many freedom lovers around the world.

As the summit ended, Reagan, who had always called the Soviet Union an "evil empire," had his arm around Gorbachev's shoulder and was calling him "friend."

Gorbachev appeared to be confident throughout the summit while Reagan, some years his senior, seemed to have trouble staying awake, not only at the opera, but during his host's speeches. At the opera, Gorbachev nudged him awake.

The Gorbachev charm had worked during the Moscow summit as perhaps never before. He had succeeded in getting the arms control treaty he wanted and had managed to change Reagan's mind about the lack of human rights in his country. Then, afterward, in the first press conference ever held by a general secretary, he said the summit had been a success, "[But] . . . we could have achieved more."

What Gorbachev hoped for was another agreement on arms control, this one a 50 percent reduction in long-range nuclear missiles. He wanted it, and apparently had the approval of the Supreme Soviet to make such an offer. But Reagan had not been prepared to move as fast on this further step in arms reduction. It became doubtful such an agreement could be made in the remaining months of Reagan's term as president. Gorbachev would have to wait and deal with the next person to occupy the White House.

Still, Gorbachev came away from the summit with much to be pleased about. He called the summit "a major event" and said its most important result was "a continuation of the dialogue that now encompasses all the issues" in Soviet-American relations.

Both Gorbachev and Reagan seemed to have gotten what they wanted. Gorbachev wanted a slowdown in the arms race to reduce defense spending that was seriously draining the Soviet economy, and the savings could be used on his domestic reform programs. Reagan, his presidency still hanging under a cloud of incompetency from the Iran-contra scandal, needed a big win to make him look successful and in command during his final months in office. An arms reduction agreement might possibly turn public favor back his way.

In London on his way home from the summit, Reagan

reported that, "Quite possibly we are beginning to take down the barriers of the postwar era; quite possibly we are entering a new era in history, a time of lasting change in the Soviet Union. We will have to see."

Political analysts studying the summit appeared to agree that Mikhail Gorbachev came out the clear winner over Ronald Reagan.

Gorbachev succeeded in winning very favorable press, even among many skeptics. They liked his style and they liked what he was doing toward arms reduction in the world, and change and reform in his country.

Was Gorbachev for real? Was he sincere and could he bring about the restructuring, the far-reaching changes in his country, that he so passionately wanted? Political analysts would give him the benefit of the doubt, for the time being. They would, like Reagan, wait and see.

But was the Cold War ended now, as some said? Had the Moscow summit melted the years of mistrust and fear that had grown out of the Stalin era at the end of World War II?

No, the Cold War was not ended, and could not after just one moderately eventful summit. After all, there was still a long way to go in ending the nuclear arms race and the progress so far was only a drop in the bucket. Only a thaw in the Cold War could be claimed, but even that was progress.

Had the "evil empire" already changed? Only time would tell.

Had Gorbachev succeeded in charming the president of the United States into no longer thinking that Gorbachev was Darth Vader?

Apparently, he had.

Chapter 12

WHO *IS* MIKHAIL GORBACHEV?

Soviet leaders are much more private people than are most American or other foreign political heads of state. They do not seem to play much and appear always to be working. So how can we learn what a world leader such as Mikhail Gorbachev really is like? For the most part, we can make presumptions based only on what others have said about him.

During the course of his first four years in office, many people met with Gorbachev. They began reporting on what they could observe about his private life, and on the kind of person he was professionally. From these observations we may be able to paint a more revealing picture of the Soviet leader.

Gorbachev and his wife, Raisa, have an apartment near the Kremlin and a lakeside home outside Moscow. Gorbachev likes to go hiking and enjoys listening to classical music. He has read widely in world literature and tries to find the time to read more literature and history. The Gorbachevs attend the ballet and the theater regularly and have taken motoring vacations in Italy and France.

Gorbachev is somewhat bald. A prominent strawberry-colored birthmark on his pate is usually airbrushed out of official photographs. He wears a hearing aid. He is a stocky man, five feet ten inches tall, and some say he looks like the American actor, Rod Steiger. He dresses in conservative, but well-tailored, dark-colored suits.

He has been described as a soft-spoken, mild-mannered man who is direct without seeming to be sharp or too aggressive. His face is often expressive, not frowning like most of his predecessors, and he has a ready smile and a good sense of humor. He usually works six days a week and puts in twelve-hour workdays.

"He's a master of words," Congressman O'Neill, now retired, said after talking with him in 1985 in Moscow. "A master of the art of politics and diplomacy. He's hard, he's tough, he's strong."

In his nomination speech on Gorbachev's behalf, Andrei Gromyko said, "Comrades, this man has a nice smile, but he's got iron teeth."

But many who have observed Gorbachev do not find in him the "killer instinct" they found in his predecessors. He has a self-confidence gained from working his way up the ranks in the Communist party.

Further observations about Gorbachev were made by a group of Soviet writers. They were unexpectedly invited by Gorbachev to meet with him in July 1986 and say whatever was on their minds. It was perhaps the first time a Soviet leader had ever done such a thing.

The four-hour meeting was held behind closed doors in Moscow and the writers said afterward that the session provided an interesting picture of Gorbachev. They were impressed by his informality and his ability to speak "off the cuff," which was rare in his predecessors. The writers also sensed his deep frustration with the slow progress of economic change in their country.

Two well-known Soviet writers, a poet and a playwright, told of their impressions meeting with Gorbachev, but did not want to be identified. Both had had difficult relations with previous general secretaries and had reputations for being somewhat critical of their leaders.

"It was a very free-ranging talk," the playwright reported. "No notes, a very conversational tone. He was thinking aloud. He was ready to hear people talk about the real situation in the country."

The poet, even more impressed, said there was, "No blah, blah, blah. He spoke very openly about negative things in the country. He just talked to us; he didn't read a report. He knew who we were. When we raised our hands to speak, he addressed us each by name. There were no aides whispering in his ear, no diagram identifying the participants." (Most past leaders would have conducted such a meeting with these aides, if it had been held at all.)

"He talked about the need to change the economy and change people's way of thinking," said the poet.

"He spoke about the slowness of change," the playwright said. "And he stressed the need to make the change irreversible."

Among other things, Gorbachev promised the writers there would be more freedom of expression, including reforms in the national theater. Directors of plays and movies could be given more freedom to express their views in their works. When one writer said that not all theater directors would welcome such change, Gorbachev said he was having the same problem with his economic reforms.

"Mediocrity does not always welcome freedom," Gorbachev said boldly. "It's easier for mediocre people to live within the framework of controls."

The day after meeting with the writers, Gorbachev spoke at the congress of the Soviet Writers' Union. One member, a poet, said, "I think Gorbachev was the most liberal person in the room."

After the conference, neither the poet nor the playwright were confident that Gorbachev's reform plans would work. "I'm optimistic, but I'm realistic," said the poet. If Gorbachev's effort to reform the economy fails, he added, "It's the death of the country."[1]

Who *is* Mikhail Gorbachev? No one knows for sure, because he is a very private person. But some things are clear from his first few years as general secretary. He is intelligent, shrewd, capable, and charming. He is an adroit politician, cool under pressure, and a man of wit. He can keep his anger or frustration under control and wait for things to turn in his favor. He is a very hard worker and dedicated to bringing about positive change for his people.

He has dreams for his country and has the determination to work for them to come true, despite enormous obstacles. But he has shown he will take risks and move more quickly toward reform if others move too slowly.

After the Moscow summit in June 1988, President Reagan praised Gorbachev as a leader interested in serious reforms.

"Today we can say with caution that we may be entering a new era of U.S. and Soviet relations," he said. "It's been a long time coming, but unlike past improvements that only saw a brief day, I think this one will have a broad and stable footing. If the Soviets want it and grow, it can and it will."

After the Moscow summit, another step toward nuclear arms control was taken by the Soviets when Gorbachev's foreign minister Eduard Shevardnadze said the Soviet Union would observe a permanent moratorium on nuclear testing, if the United States did the same.

Something extraordinary happened in Moscow late in June. Soviet citizens watched on live television as nearly five thousand delegates from all across the country attended an historic conference of the Communist party. What made the meeting so special was the degree of openness and the calls for change that were made.

Leading the crusade for change was General Secretary Gorbachev, but his strong defense of glasnost and perestroika was soon echoed by many other Party leaders and delegates. Previously unheard-of debate turned the conference into the liveliest, most open party meeting anyone could remember.

Gorbachev urged both conservatives and reformers to unite for the good of the country. He repeatedly warned that its future depended on their embrace of restructuring the economic and political systems that had brought about decades of stagnation.

"I will tell you outright," Gorbachev said passionately, "if we do not reform the political system, all our initiatives, the whole massive task we have undertaken, will grind to a halt."[2]

It was Gorbachev's most visible and vocal cry yet for change and reform. By the end of the four days, it was obvious he had emerged with strong support from the delegates, though there was still some opposition from older, more conservative party leaders. Yet it encouraged Gorbachev to say in his closing address that the conference had opened the way to a democratic image of socialism and he appeared to be more confident that he would be given the support he needed to implement his program for perestroika.

Perhaps the most far-reaching proposal Gorbachev made

at the conference was his plan for a major restructuring of the Soviet government. The delegates approved six resolutions toward achieving this as well as other political, social, and economic reform.

One proposal called for a new national legislature that would elect a president who would have the authority to manage both foreign and domestic policy. Gorbachev might, then, in addition to being general secretary, be president as well. And all Party officials would be limited to two five-year terms. This would help end the long careers of the elderly conservative Party leaders and bring younger people with fresh ideas into the political system.

Gorbachev had succeeded in spreading his crusade not only further within the Party, but beyond the Kremlin and into the homes and minds of Soviet citizens. There could be no going back, he told them. Now, for their survival, they had to go forward into glasnost and perestroika.

By the middle of his fourth year in office, Gorbachev had made extraordinary strides toward getting the reforms his country would need to embrace in order to pull itself up out of decades of stagnation. Only time would tell, if Gorbachev remained in power long enough to see his dreams for his country come true.

Most American and other free-world leaders agreed, it would be bad and even dangerous if Gorbachev did not succeed, and the Soviet Union went back into isolation and further economic, industrial, and agricultural difficulties. Those conditions breed military aggression.

The "have nots" make war. Those who "have" a decent standard of living are content with peace. So it was in the West's best interests to help Gorbachev succeed.

Gorbachev appeared to be the right leader at the right time for his people.

Mikhail Sergeyevich Gorbachev 1931-

1931 Mikhail Sergeyevich Gorbachev is born March 2 in Privolnoye, U.S.S.R. Thomas Alva Edison dies. Wiley Post and Harold Gatty are first to fly around the world. Ernest Lawrence invents the cyclotron, or "atom smasher."

1932 Famine in the Soviet Union. Amelia Earhart becomes first woman to fly solo across the Atlantic Ocean.

1933 Famine continues in Soviet Union. Franklin Delano Roosevelt inaugurated 32nd president of the United States. U.S. recognizes U.S.S.R. Adolf Hitler appointed German chancellor. Japan withdraws from the League of Nations. The first concentration camps are erected by the Nazis in Germany and the persecution of Jews begins.

1934 U.S.S.R. joins League of Nations. Hitler is elected führer (leader) of Germany.

1935 Hitler and Benito Mussolini of Italy proclaim Rome-Berlin axis. American humorist Will Rogers dies in plane crash. Amelia Earhart becomes first woman to fly solo across the Pacific.

1936 Joseph Stalin begins political purges in U.S.S.R., which continue until 1939. "Stalin Constitution" is put into effect. In U.S.A., social security goes into effect.

1937 Amelia Earhart is lost on flight over Pacific Ocean.

1938 Germany annexes Austria. Bingo becomes a new rage and fund-raiser in U.S.

1939 Gorbachev begins primary school. Hitler invades Poland, beginning of World War II. Germany annexes Czechoslovakia. Soviet-Nazi nonaggression pact is signed. U.S.S.R. invades Finland.

1940 Germany invades Denmark, Norway, Holland, Belgium, and Luxembourg. Finland surrenders. France falls to Nazi troops. Nazi bombing of London and "The Battle of Britain" begins. Germany, Italy, and Japan sign military and economic pact.

1941 German armies invade U.S.S.R. and reach Moscow. Siege of Leningrad begins. Franklin Roosevelt begins unprecedented third term as president of U.S. Japan attacks Pearl Harbor; U.S. declares war on Japan. U.S. declares war on Germany and Italy. Gorbachev's father joins Soviet army. Nazis invade Stavropol, 200 miles from Privolnoye, Gorbachev's village.

1942 Gorbachev drops out of primary school to work in war effort. Battle of Stalingrad begins. The murder of millions of Jews in Nazi gas chambers begins.

1943 Gorbachev resumes primary school education. Teheran conference of Allied leaders.

1944 Gorbachev begins pre-secondary school. Battle of Stalingrad ends. United Nations is established by delegates from the U.S., U.S.S.R., Great Britain, and China.

1945 Gorbachev starts working summers at local tractor station. Allied leaders meet at Yalta. Roosevelt dies and is succeeded by Vice-President Harry S. Truman. Germany surrenders. U.S. drops two atom bombs on Japan. Japan surrenders, ending World War II.

1946 Soviet armies overrun Eastern Europe. An "iron curtain" divides East and West, and a "cold war" of suspicion and rivalry begins between the U.S.S.R. and the U.S.

1947 Gorbachev begins secondary school. United Nations proposes to partition Palestine into Arab and Jewish states; Jews accept plan, Arabs reject it.

1948 Soviets begin blockade of West Berlin. Jewish state of Israel is proclaimed. Arab armies invade Israel.

1949 Gorbachev is awarded Order of the Red Banner of Labor and becomes candidate for Communist party membership. North Atlantic Treaty Organization (NATO) is formed. President Truman begins second term. Armistice is signed in Arab-Israeli War.

1950 Gorbachev graduates from secondary school with silver medal award and enters Moscow State University. Korean War begins. President Truman authorizes work on hydrogen bomb; U.S. physicists protest against it being used as a "weapon of war."

1953 Stalin dies. Nikita Khrushchev becomes sole leader of U.S.S.R. Korean War ends. In U.S., Dwight David Eisenhower becomes 34th president.

1955 Gorbachev is graduated from Law Faculty of Moscow State University, returns to Stavropol to work for Komsomol (Young Communist League), and marries Raisa Titorenko. Soviet jet planes fire on U.S. naval patrol plane on routine flight over Bering Strait; Soviets regret incident.

1956 Gorbachev becomes secretary of Stavropol city Komsomol Committee. Daughter Irina is born. Khrushchev condemns isolationist policies of Stalin and his "cult of personality," and opens Soviet Union to foreign trade, journalists, and some tourists. Second Arab-Israeli War begins.

1957 Arab-Israeli War ends. Gorbachev works as first deputy chief of propaganda for Stavropol region (until 1961). President Eisenhower begins second term. Soviet scientists launch into space the first artificial man-made earth-orbiting satellite, *Sputnik I*, then a month later, a second, bearing a small female dog, named Laika.

1958 Egypt and Syria unite, forming United Arab Republic (UAR). U.S. duplicates Soviet space achievements by launching its first space satellite, *Explorer I*, and later sends a squirrel monkey into space in a *Jupiter* missile.

1960 Tensions escalate between the U.S. and Soviet Union when a U.S. weather research plane is shot down after straying into Soviet-Afghanistan air territory. As a result, a planned summit meeting between Khrushchev and Eisenhower is called off.

1961 John F. Kennedy becomes president of the United States and authorizes the Peace Corps. Syria withdraws from UAR. The Soviet Union resumes nuclear testing, despite a moratorium, and explodes a bomb in the Arctic. The Berlin Wall is built preventing East Berliners from going into West Berlin. Soviet cosmonaut Yuri Gagarin becomes the first man in space.

1962 Lt. Col. John H. Glenn, Jr. becomes the first American to orbit the earth. The Vietnam War begins and continues to 1975. The U.S. objects to the placement of Soviet missiles in Cuba.

1963 Gorbachev becomes chief of the agricultural department for the Stavropol region. Kennedy is assassinated and Vice-President Lyndon B. Johnson becomes president of the U.S. The U.S. and Soviet Union agree to end problem over Cuba when the Soviets withdraw missile sites there. The U.S., Soviet Union, and Great Britain sign a treaty banning nuclear weapons tests, except those underground. The U.S. and U.S.S.R. agree to establish a "hot line" between Washington and Moscow to speed communications in a crisis, such as in the Cuban confrontation.

1964 The Civil Rights Act of 1964 is signed by President Johnson. Khrushchev is removed from power. Aleksei Kosygin becomes first secretary of the Communist Party Central Committee.

1968 Soviet troops invade Czechoslovakia. The first U.S.-U.S.S.R. consular treaty since the Russian Revolution is signed. Richard M. Nixon is elected president of the United States. The Rev. Martin Luther King, Jr. is killed by a sniper's bullet. Senator Robert F. Kennedy is assassinated. U.S. astronauts Neil Armstrong and Edwin Aldrin become the first men to walk on the moon.

1969 The Soviet Union and China fight limited battles in border disputes.

1970 Gorbachev is named a deputy to the Soviet of the Union within the Supreme Soviet.

1971 Gorbachev becomes a member of the Communist Party Central Committee and begins heading Party delegation trips abroad.

1972 The U.S.S.R. and U.S. sign a treaty to limit production of nuclear weapons.

1973 The U.S.S.R. and U.S. sign an arms limitation agreement. Egypt and Syria attack Israel.

1974 Gorbachev becomes chairman of the Komsomol.

1976 Gorbachev's father dies.

1977 Jimmy Carter becomes president of the U.S. Leonid Brezhnev becomes chairman of the Presidium of the Supreme Soviet. The U.S.S.R. and U.S. sign the SALT I (Strategic Arms Limitation Treaty) agreement.

1978 Gorbachev becomes secretary of agriculture. Carter and heads of Israel and Egypt hold talks toward ending the Arab-Israeli War.

1979 Gorbachev becomes a nonvoting member of the Politburo. A peace treaty ends the Arab-Israeli War. The U.S.S.R. and U.S. sign the SALT II agreement. The Soviet Union invades Afghanistan. The U.S. Congress refuses to ratify the SALT II agreement in protest against the invasion of Afghanistan by the Soviets.

1980 Kosygin retires and is replaced by Nikoly Tikhonov. The Olympic Games are held in Moscow, but are boycotted by the U.S.

1981 Ronald Reagan becomes 40th president of the U.S.

1982 Leonid Brezhnev dies and is succeeded by Yuri Andropov. Gorbachev becomes Andropov's right-hand man.

1984 Gorbachev supervises Andropov's limited reform programs in some small industries. Andropov dies and is succeeded by Konstantin Chernenko. Gorbachev becomes chairman of the Communist party's ideology and economic committees, then chairman of the foreign affairs committee of the Supreme Soviet. The U.S.S.R. declines to take part in the Olympic Games held in Los Angeles, California. In December, Gorbachev leads a delegation to London and meets with Prime Minister Margaret Thatcher of Great Britain.

1985 Chernenko dies and Gorbachev becomes general secretary. At age 54, he is the youngest Soviet leader since Stalin succeeded Lenin in 1924. Gorbachev urges the Communist party and other government leaders to support a sweeping new program of change and openness including more Socialist self-government by the people and improving industrial and farm production. He favors arms reduction but opposes President Reagan's SDI, calling it a dangerous militarization of space. Gorbachev and President Reagan meet in a November summit in Geneva, Switzerland, and agree to keep ongoing dialogue.

1986 Gorbachev spells out his policies for change and reform. A nuclear power plant disaster occurs in Chernobyl, a city in the Ukrainian region of the U.S.S.R. Gorbachev meets with President Reagan for arms control talks in Reykjavik, Iceland. Gorbachev suggests reducing nuclear arsenals by 50 percent, but Reagan refuses to negotiate on his SDI, and the talks break down.

1987 Gorbachev returns to domestic reform and a purge of Stalin begins. The U.S. conducts a nuclear test in violation of test ban treaties and the Soviets retaliate by exploding a nuclear device in Karakhstan, a remote Soviet region. New arms reduction offers by Gorbachev are made to reduce medium-range missiles without concessions on SDI. Matthias Rust, 19, flies his private plane from West Germany to Moscow, landing in Red Square without being detected, causing a security scandal that Gorbachev turns to his advantage. Gorbachev calls for election reforms, more freedom for the Soviet press, and promises the people they will not suffer if they speak openly and criticize their bosses and leaders. Gorbachev "vanishes" for nearly seven weeks in late summer, reappears in September saying he took a vacation, wrote a speech, and concluded work on a new book. The book, *Perestroika*, sets forth his plans for a total restructuring of the Soviet system, especially its economy. Gorbachev and Reagan meet at summit in Washington, D.C., and sign treaty to eliminate medium-range nuclear missiles. *Time* magazine puts Gorbachev on cover as "Man of the Year."

1988 Electoral reform is negotiated by Communist party officials. Soviets begin dismantling part of their intermediate-range arsenal in East Germany. In April, Soviets agree to start pulling their troops out of Afghanistan giving it up as a "no-win" war. Farm reform begins with higher status for agricultural cooperatives. A dissidents' meeting to start a new political party is broken up. Gorbachev visits Yugoslavia and announces that Soviet control over its satellite countries will be lessened and they will be allowed more independence. U.S. Senate ratifies intermediate-range missile treaty. Reagan goes to Moscow in June for fourth summit with Gorbachev. Reagan criticizes human rights violations in U.S.S.R., then does a switch and blames them not on the Soviet government but bureaucratic redtape. Gorbachev charms Reagan into no longer thinking of U.S.S.R. as an "evil empire." Gorbachev's hopes of achieving another arms agreement at the Moscow summit, calling for a 50 percent reduction in long-range nuclear missiles, are not realized. He indicates he will continue to work for this, with Reagan or the next United States president. As a result of the Moscow summit, some think the Cold War that began in the Stalin era after World War II has ended, while others more cautious say there is only a thaw. Gorbachev appears to be on his way to getting most of the reforms he says his country must have to end decades of stagnation. In July, in a strong showing of power, Gorbachev overhauls the Soviet political system. Reforms result in removal of many of his old conservative critics, replacing them with men of his own thinking. Also, Gorbachev becomes his country's president as well as the Communist Party's general secretary, increasing his power base. In October, Gorbachev reshuffles leadership of the Russian Federation, largest of the Soviet Union's 15 republics, further tightening his control over major party and government organizations to enable him to push through his reforms. In November, Gorbachev pledges to work with George Bush, victor in the U.S. presidential elections, toward further independence from Soviet authority. Gorbachev walks a fine line with the Soviet satellite countries, encouraging openness and reform, but insisting that Estonia and other Soviet states must continue to toe the line. He calls for a special commission to study the relationship between the Soviet republics and the central government in Moscow. In December, Gorbachev wins overwhelming endorsement of a series of radical changes in government structure and electoral laws from the Supreme Soviet. Near year's end, Gorbachev visits New York and addresses the United Nations, announcing that the Soviet Union will reduce its armed forces by about 10 percent and will remove some of its forces from East Germany and its borders with China. He meets briefly with Reagan and president-elect Bush, and they pledge mutual cooperation for peace. Gorbachev's announcement of armed forces reductions for defense rather than attack against Western Europe are regarded as a very hopeful sign that his policies for reform and peace are moving forward. But his trip is cut short by a devastating earthquake in the Soviet satellite country of Armenia where tens of thousands are killed.

NOTES

Chapter 2
1. Janet G. Vaillant and John Richards II, *From Russia to USSR: A Narrative and Documentary History* (White Plains, New York: Longman Inc., 1985), 229.

Chapter 3
1. Roy Medvedev, *Let History Judge* Copyright © by Roy Medvedev.
2. "Gorbachev knew poverty as a child, mother says," Associated Press (July 18, 1988).

Chapter 4
1. *Current Biography Yearbook 1985* (Bronx, New York: The H.W. Wilson Company, 1985, 1986), 153.

Chapter 5
1. "'Glasnost': Moscow's New Rallying Cry," *Newsweek* (January, 5, 1987), 20.
2. Ibid.

Chapter 6
1. Vaillant and Richards, *From Russia to USSR: A Narrative and Documentary History*, 305.

2. Mikhail S. Gorbachev, *A Time for Peace* (New York: Richardson & Steirman, 1985), 19-20.
3. Ibid., 73-5.
4. Ibid., 81.
5. Ibid., 82.
6. Mikhail S. Gorbachev, *The Coming Century of Peace* (New York: Richardson & Steirman, 1986), 185.
7. Ibid.
8. Ibid., 186-87.
9. Ibid., 187.
10. Ibid., 189.
11. Ibid., 201.
12. Gorbachev, *A Time for Peace*, 124.
13. Ibid., 186.
14. Ibid., 222.
15. Gorbachev, *The Coming Century of Peace*, 27.
16. Ibid., 156.

Chapter 7
1. Gorbachev, *The Coming Century of Peace*, 11.
2. Ibid., 11-12.
3. Ibid., 12.
4. Ibid.
5. Ibid., 14.
6. Ibid.
7. Ibid., 17.
8. "A soft-talk, tough-talk, Kremlin defense" by Stanley N. Wellborn, *U.S. News & World Report* (May 26, 1986), 4.
9. "Chernobyl takes glow off the famous Gorbachev 'charm'" by Dimitri K. Simes, *The Christian Science Monitor* (May 14, 1987).
10. "Text of Reagan's speech on summit," United Press International (October 14, 1986).
11. "Deadlock in Iceland," *Newsweek* (October 20, 1986), 20.

Chapter 8
1. "Soviets vow to resume nuclear tests in '87 if U.S. doesn't stop" by Thom Shanker, *Chicago Tribune* (December 19, 1986).
2. "Soviets offer missile plan" by Thom

Shanker, *Chicago Tribune* (March 1, 1987).

Chapter 9
1. "Soviet magazine tosses out idea 'like a hooligan,' editor says" by Paul Quinn-Judge, *The Christian Science Monitor* (February 20, 1987).
2. "Gorbachev pushes for radical change" by Paul Quinn-Judge, *The Christian Science Monitor* (March 10, 1987).
3. "Gorbachev confronts rumors" by Thom Shanker, *Chicago Tribune* (May 21, 1987).
4. "Gorbachev: Reforms resisted within party," Associated Press (April 17, 1987).
5. "Glasnost: 'There's no turning back,'" an interview with Andrei Sakharov and his wife Yelena Bonner conducted by Editor-in-Chief Mortimer B. Zuckerman, *U.S. News & World Report* (April 20, 1987).

Chapter 10
1. "Kissinger: How to Deal With Gorbachev" by Dr. Henry A. Kissinger, *Newsweek* (March 2, 1987).
2. "A second 'revolution' in the Soviet Union" by Walter C. Clemens Jr., *The Christian Science Monitor* (January 15, 1987).
3. "Red Faces in Red Square," *Newsweek* (June 8, 1987), 36.
4. "Gorbachev takes on the generals" by Jeff Trimble, *U.S. News & World Report* (June 15, 1987).

Chapter 11
1. "Gorbachev seeks sugar for a lemon" by Jim Gallagher, *Chicago Tribune* (November 29, 1987).
2. "Filmmaker: Many Soviets oppose reform," Reuters (December 24, 1987).

Chapter 12
1. "Soviet writers tell of private meeting with Gorbachev" by Paul Quinn-Judge, *The Christian Science Monitor* (July 18, 1986).
2. "Moscow's Free-for-All, *Newsweek* (July 11, 1988).

INDEX- *Page numbers in boldface type indicate illustrations.*

About the Author

Walter Olesky writes adventure novels for preteens and teenagers including a new Hardy Boys book, *Shield of Fear*, and an Indiana Jones-type adventure, *Headhunters of the Dagger of Death*. He also writes nonfiction books for those ages including several for Childrens Press: *Miracles of Genetics*, *Experiments with Heat*, *The Video Revolution*, and *Lasers*. A bachelor, he lives near Chicago with his black Lab, Max, and they enjoy Frisbee tossing along the lakefront and visiting with friends.